I0069862

Also by Gabrielle Dahms

The Real Estate Investor Manuals
How Trends Make You A Smarter Investor
Finding Profitable Deals
The Art and Science of Real Estate Negotiation
Investing in Real Estate in Your Self-Directed IRA

Watch for more at https://www.BooksmartPress.com.

Table of Contents

Investing in Real Estate in your Self-Directed IRA

Secrets to Retiring Wealthy and Leaving a Legacy

The Real Estate Investor Manuals, Volume IV

Disclaimer: Data provided here is deemed to be accurate but NOT guaranteed. The contents imply neither legal nor financial advice. Always thoroughly evaluate the facts relating to your specific circumstances. Neither Booksmart Press LLC and/or Gabrielle Dahms guarantee results. The self-directed IRA landscape continues to change and depends on laws, statues and rulings. All investments carry risks which must be assessed through due diligence and/or by consulting appropriate professionals. The author neither implicitly nor explicitly endorses any third party, company, custodian, or product mentioned in the book. Always seek appropriate counsel and do your homework. The author is not responsible for any liability, loss, or risk incurred resulting from the use of any of the information contained in this book - now or in the future.

All opinions and remaining spelling or grammatical mistakes are those of the author.

This is a non-fiction work.

Copyright © Booksmart Press LLC 2021

All rights reserved.

This book or any portion of it may not be reproduced or used in any manner whatsoever without the express prior written permission of the publisher except for use of brief quotations in a book review. For permission requests, email the author at realestatemanuals@gmail.com.

Book Cover by 100Covers

Published by Booksmart Press LLC

ISBN Paperback 978-1-7331473-7-8

ISBN eBook 978-1-7331473-8-5

ISBN audio book 978-1-7331473-9-2

Library of Congress Control Number: 2021921733

Publisher's Cataloging-in-Publication data

Names: Dahms, Gabrielle.

Title: / by Gabrielle Dahms.

Series: The Real Estate Investor Manuals

Description: Includes bibliographical references and indexes. | Cheyenne, WY: Booksmart Press, 2021.

Identifiers: ISBN: 978-1-7331473-7-8 (pbk.) | 978-1-7331473-8-5 (ebook) | 978-1-7331473-9-2 (audio)

Subjects: LCSH Real Estate Business. | Real property. | Real estate agents. | Negotiation in business. | House buying. | House selling. | Commercial real estate. | BISAC BUSINESS & ECONOMICS/ Real Estate / General | BUSINESS & ECONOMICS/ Negotiating | BUSINESS & ECONOMICS/ Conflict Resolution & Mediation

Classification: LCC HD1379 .D24 2020 | DDC 333.33—dc23

Other Books in This Series

$$\Omega$$

How Trends Make You A Smarter Investor (Vol. I)
    Finding Profitable Deals (Vol. II)
    The Art and Science of Real Estate Negotiation (Vol. III)
    Upcoming book subjects in this series include:

    International Real Estate
    Affordable Housing
    Market analysis

    Paperback and hardcopy editions are available from Ingram Sparks and KDP.
    eBooks are available through your favorite eBook retailers.
    Audio Books are available via FindAway Voices.

Join our mailing list here.
www.sdirarealestateinvesting.com[1]
We detest SPAM and do not send it.
All you receive are updates of our publications.

---

1. http://www.sdirarealestateinvesting.com

What Readers say about

the other books in the series

Ω

How Trends Make You a Smarter Investor

... this book was easy and entertaining to read - almost like a novel - quite an achievement in such a topic I would think of as "dry". Nonetheless, Gabrielle Dahms covers the essential steps in real estate investment. The Real Estate Investment Manuals series takes a holistic approach to investment. – ☆☆☆☆☆ Kalavan

What I enjoyed most about this book is how the author was able to break down a complex subject into understandable terms and strategies. I have been a real estate agent for some time and know that real estate investment is a complicated process as there is so much to consider. In the Real Estate Investing Manuals, Ms. Dahms was able to explain all the steps concisely and clearly. – ☆☆☆☆☆ L. Martini

This book has a wonderful section on 21st century topics in real estate, such as cryptocurrency, the gig economy, and the opportunities it creates, and the current effects of technology in general on the real estate industry. I found the book's focus on how real estate shapes our society very interesting. For instance, it addresses green homes and community-focused real estate. - ☆☆☆☆☆ D. Cale

Finding Profitable Deals

Many of us know that buying and selling real estate is a goldmine! The issue for me has been understanding the basics and where the deals are! So many real estate books I've picked up are sleepers! I just can't get through them. But not Gabrielle Dahms' book! I couldn't put it down! It was a fast and easy read and now, I am filled with inspiration and knowledge that I can use right now!! What a super resource!! Now I feel like I'm on my way to Real Estate Wealth! – ☆☆☆☆☆ A customer

... very beneficial for those looking to just buy a family home. The author gives a surprising amount of information about what types of investments are out there. The author's insight makes me feel I can make the best purchase without the fear of losing my investment if I need to resell. I am looking forward to using the tips I learned to good use, thanks. - ★★★★★ J. Maxon

The Art and Science of Real Estate Negotiation

The author does a great job illustrating the tactics, skills and tips to succeed in real estate negotiations. I have read many other negotiation books, with this being the only one dedicated to real estate. Very good from that perspective and would highly recommend it. – ★★★★★ A Gayl

The principal problem of any exchange of goods is the assignment of value. We soon notice that there is a difference between assigned and intrinsic value; in other words value is an evanescent concept and easily becomes detached from the exchange.

That is why Gabrielle Dahms book, "The Art and Science of Real Estate Negotiation" is so welcome. In a succinct 200 odd pages, she sets out the indispensable steps any person coming into real estate negotiation needs to know.

The main theme of the book, the mantra that stands out for a Real Estate Professional is :"Do your homework". No two deals are identical, and the perception of value is the main variable. The professional realtor has an eye and and a feeling for all the moving parts of the possible deal, and is an indispensable support in any transaction.

Gabrielle Dahms brings her deep knowledge of the industry and its methodologies and sets them out, in clear and simple language, for the reader to use and, yes, enjoy! – ★★★★★ A. C.

DEDICATION

Ω

I am grateful to colleagues, friends, family and clients for their support and love.

Bonuses

Ω

Bonus Materials That Accompany This Book

✓ Fillable Return-on-Investment Calculator

✓ Due Diligence Master List

✓ Custodian Comparison Sheet

✓ Real estate investing Presentations & Videos

Claim them at www.sdirarealestateinvesting.com[1]

---

1. http://www.sdirarealestateinvesting.com

Why this book?

Ω

If you, like me, have ever seen an 80-year-old working at Walmart, Costco or other retailers, you most likely have encountered someone with insufficient retirement dollars. It breaks my heart to witness this, even though I know some claim that they like the social interaction of the job. Perhaps so, but wouldn't joining a social club or visiting a park or volunteering do the same?

The necessity for a job long after people in most developed countries enjoy their lives, evidences the conundrum in which these retirees find themselves. Of course, anyone who desires to work when they are 80 or 90 years old is free to do so. But if you would rather enjoy your life by traveling, seeing your family, playing golf or bridge, or doing anything else to occupy your time and keep yourself mentally well, this book is for you.

The need to plan for the golden years comes years and decades before to ensure sufficient funds for that time. A good and adaptable plan allows for a great start to financial security and wealth. Many people, myself included, found themselves battered by the Great Recession. We limped away with portfolios now worth a fraction of their values before the crash. The Great Recession even the financially wiped out some of us. We believed we had a plan, though most of it usually was hands off and we discovered that the financial markets were out of our control.

This may mean having to start over or starting late. Now, our focus is more on a plan that allows for more control over the investments we choose. Please find the courage to start or to start again as soon as possible. This book advocates doing so via a self-directed IRA, which allows you to invest and save for retirement with alternative investments, including real estate. Savvy financial planning for your nest egg via an SD-IRA enables you to enjoy your life when you choose to retire—with much more control over your investments and better returns than Wall Street offers. And while time remains an important component in building your portfolio, real estate investments can supercharge your account.

Sail into retirement with full coffers and enjoy it. Take advantage of economic opportunities to generate income and security and become financially free. The appeal of securing one's life and lifestyle and building wealth for the future lures. To do so even becomes necessary, given the immense social and economic changes of the past fifty years. Here is what I mean by that.

Pensions are almost non-existent today. Retirement planning has shifted from companies and the corporate sector to every American planning for himself. Yes, companies offer 401 (k) plans to qualified employees, but such plans invest in stocks, bonds and mutual funds, which return between 3% and 8% on average. [i] Such returns, though better than a CD with your bank nets, are paltry when considering that inflation eats a fair amount of the returns. [ii]

But there is a better, more profitable way which we discuss in this book. It is the self-directed IRA, a legal instrument intended to help and encourage Americans to retire in style. You will discover how self-directed IRAs work, what investment options you have, how to get started, and much more.

Self-directed IRAs have been on my horizon for over two decades. They continue to be less well known than they should be, though the public is now more aware of them. These powerful accounts can help you grow your retirement funds in sometimes exponential ways.

A whole industry has grown around them since the late 1990s and early 2000s. The accounts came into existence in 1997 and only a few custodians held and serviced them then. Custodians differ from brokerage firms, something explained in chapter 5. Over the past 20 years, more self-directed IRA custodians have entered the field, a trend that is likely to continue. And that is good news for consumers.

However, confusion persists about the powerful growth vehicles self-directed IRAs represent. You will learn why that is the case and gain clarity to propel you to action. Buckle up if confusion surrounds how self-directed IRAs work or about how to proceed. Let's clear the smoke and gain clarity on how to proceed. I will show options and ways to overcome whatever obstacles might be in your path to the retirement of your dreams.

Another important note is that this book specifically addresses investing in real estate through self-directed IRAs. Several reasons drive this focus. I am a real estate investor and broker who uses self-directed IRAs and who has spread the word about these accounts for almost two decades.

In a high cost of living and high real estate value area like the San Francisco Bay Area (where I live), being able to afford property is perhaps something that occupies many investors' and would be investors' minds. Even realtors and investors like myself have to find money to fund properties and deals.

Some of us may or may not qualify for conventional loans on properties and therefore have to be more creative in how to fund investments. When I first came to real estate some 20 years ago from a research and marketing background, I knew next to nothing about the subject. I quickly learned that access to money, either as financing or having cash, is the name of the game in real estate. I researched ways to finance property and eventually came across the powerful instrument that this book is about: self-directed IRAs. Self-directed IRAs are specific to investments, including real estate investments. The IRS has rules on them.

As already mentioned, these instruments were then much less well known than they are today. My aim became to educate as many people as possible so that they too could benefit from these retirement vehicles blessed by the United States government. Simultaneously, I continued to build my real estate portfolio via my self-directed IRA account.

During that time, I found that two essential components drive real estate investing: finding the money and finding the property, often referred to as the "deal." Many people dream about real estate investing but get stuck with the *finding the money* part. Well, the good news is that self-directed IRAs can take care of that component because you may roll over retirement account funds you already have into such accounts.

You may already have either a 401 (k) or an IRA, neither of which allows for real estate investments them in their current form. You will learn how to shift to a truly self-directed IRA to do just that. Once the SD-IRA is established, finding the right property and investing in it grows the account.

As you can see, finding the money and the deals clearly stand in relationship to one another. The book discusses both. It provides fundamentals and pertinent examples, so that you gain confidence in self-directed IRAs and get started. The words of Plato, Athens' great philosopher, *the beginning is the most important part of the work.*

But back to this book: it serves as a guide to assess whether setting up such an account is the right path for you, and if so, how to get started as quickly as possible. The adage that time is money applies in this case. The context is that time is a finite resource none of us gets back, and the more time anyone has in investing, the better. More on that later.

Much of the information in this book comes from years of experience in real estate and in life. However, I am neither a lawyer nor a financial consultant and therefore neither offer nor imply any legal or financial advice. Although you could consult with your CPA or attorney about self-directed IRAs, you may find that you know more than these professionals after you read this book. How to proceed should that be the case is another subject we will address later.

Real estate investing is a popular topic just as much as it is a popular investment option for SD-IRAs. The book breaks down real estate categories, their requirements, due diligence and management in SD-IRA accounts. As already mentioned, what you are about to read only applies to real estate investments.

For other allowable investment categories, and for financial, tax and legal advice, please read other books about SD-IRAs. Several excellent books about the topic exist. Articles and books about this powerful investment mechanism and vehicle are also more readily available. Many such books discuss the mechanics, such as setting up the account, rolling over funds into the account from other retirement accounts, tax implications, and briefly addressing allowable investments for such accounts. Consult the bibliography for some of them.

If you want to be financially secure in your retirement years, this book is for you. If you are looking for a better way to grow your investment performance, this book is for you. Whether you already have a plan in place and want to improve upon it, or whether you're just getting started and need pertinent information to guide you, this book is for you. And even if you currently have little to no savings for retirement and feel dejected by that fact, this book is for you.

Let's get started, shall we?

Chapter 1: Supercharge Your Retirement Funds

Ω

Start from wherever you are and with whatever you've got.
— Jim Rohn

Real estate investing in your SD-IRA

What SD-IRAs are

Real estate investing in a self-directed IRA (SD-IRA) is the subject matter. If you've never heard of an SD-IRA or thought you already had one in which you can only invest in stocks, bonds, ETFs, and mutual funds, you are not alone. The next several chapters demystify these instruments.

SD-IRAs are specialty accounts, set up by the United States tax code. The term "self-directed" refers to the account holder's ability to direct which investments the account holds. By that definition, all IRAs are self-directed and that is why your brokerage claims that your IRA with them is just that.

However, regular brokerage IRAs that invest funds into stocks, bonds, ETS, mutual funds, and money markets offer these products only. Because the investor decides which of the options to invest in, they are *self-directed*. If you ask the same brokerage to invest your funds into all assets permitted by law, the broker will tell you they cannot accommodate this.

A truly self-directed IRA, then, is an account that allows you to invest in assets the law permits. Such investments include so-called alternative investments. One of them is real estate, the focus of this book. Chapters 6, 7, and 8 delineate real estate investment options and how to screen them.

Confusing, huh?

To re-iterate, brokerage houses call their accounts self-directed because the customer can choose which investments to purchase and hold, but only brokerage house products are on offer. The investment options are stocks, bonds, ETFs, and mutual funds.

They do not include real estate investments other than REITs which trade like stocks. For REITs, the investment is in a company, not in actual real estate. REIT investors do not own a piece of the company's real estate holdings.

Please don't misunderstand me. Stocks, bonds and mutual funds can serve investors well. Freshly minted millionaires and billionaires emerge from the stock market just as they do from real estate markets. Interestingly, I am unaware of such individuals coming from mutual and bond investing.

One reason the confusion about which accounts are self-directed accounts persists is that brokerage houses make money on the investment products they sell. If you decide to move that money to a custodian that allows you alternative investing, the brokerage house loses your capital and your business, at least to the extent you move assets and money. That clearly lies outside the brokerage house interests. While your broker cannot prevent you from moving your money to a custodian specialized in alternative investments, the broker can resist such moves.

Only IRA custodians (trust companies) who specialize in accounts that allow for non-traditional assets as investments will enable you to take advantage of investing your money into real estate. These custodians are specialty operators who handle real estate, private placement, note investing, and precious metal investing in your IRA.

Unlike brokerage houses, custodians make their money with fees on the account and the transactions. They have no products to sell, meaning they receive no commissions on the investments you choose for the accounts. However, in recent years, custodians like Equity Trust have shown companies that offer investments to their clients on their website. They may well get some compensation from those companies once you direct an investment to them.

Back to a self-directed IRA that accommodates real estate investing: truly self-directed IRAs allow investors to hold assets such as

> ➤ **Multi-family properties**
> ➤ **Single-family homes**
> ➤ **Tax liens**
> ➤ **Land**
> ➤ **Mortgage notes**
> ➤ **Businesses**
> ➤ **Private Placements**

No matter which of these options the investor chooses, it must be for investment. The IRS has specific rules on what qualifies as an investment and what does not. That means you cannot own your own home or the home of anyone related to you in your self-directed IRA.

The United States government, specifically the IRS, also protects against anyone going after these accounts. Predators cannot obtain judgments against these accounts. SD-IRA accounts do not appear in public records. Maintain the integrity of your SD-IRA by taking title correctly, which means never taking title to any asset in your own name. Assets are titled to the account, not to you.

After I just told you this, please be aware that your state may have laws on the books that affect how safe your SD-IRA is to protect you from creditors and judgements. Although custodians may be an initial resource for you, they can never provide the full picture. Please check with your attorney about this issue.

How well SD-IRAs are protected is state specific and layered on top of federal rules and laws. This subject is beyond this book. However, since I am in California, please be aware that 401(k)s carry better protection than IRAs in California. In the case of a personal injury lawsuit against you, a court may assign assets from an IRA to satisfy a judgment. [iii]

Real estate investing in an SD-IRA gives you control over your investments and the potential for excellent returns. They are fantastic tools to get you to the retirement you deserve after many years of contributing to the U.S. economy. If you already have a traditional IRA, a Roth IRA, or a 401(k), you are familiar with the structure of these accounts. Any IRA is a retirement account set up by an individual.

A person can have more than one IRA account, but the annual allowed contribution must be the total contributed to any such account. It cannot be more. For example, you could contribute $3000 to one of your IRAs and $3000 to your other IRA. That totals your annual contribution limit of $6000 if you are younger than 50 years. The contribution limit sits at $7000 for those over 50 years old.

While contributions alone are unlikely to make you rich, wise investments in the account will. Your decisions about how to leverage the dollars in your account drive its value.

The Power of SD-IRAs

You may already be a homeowner. If you are, you understand the power of leverage. Leverage is the ability to control an asset and even borrow against it while putting up a fraction of your own money. That is what happens when you take out a mortgage. In that way, you gain financial advantage and power through good debt. [iv]

In effect, this is a smart use of other people's money (OPM). However, you can also leverage time, knowledge, expertise and other resources, which is good news for those who lack sufficient cash reserves.

Many Proptech companies and start-ups aim to make home buying and investing easier by systematic application of technology. Imagine how powerful it is to see options populate on your screen with a few keystrokes. The entire process potentially saves you time and money. It makes your life easier.

Well, consider self-directed IRA investing with leverage in mind. A few examples of this include taking out a non-recourse loan to buy property, optioning property or its underlying paper, lending money to other investors, real estate syndications, and crowdfunding. When you invest in your SD-IRA in this way, your ability to hold multiple assets and to increase your returns expands. More on this later.

The power of investing in real estate in self-directed IRAs lies in the immense growth potential. Roth IRAs hold significant advantages for a high dollar value portfolio because the account grows tax free. In contrast, traditional IRAs eventually incur taxes, though the hope is that the account holder will presumably pay taxes in a lower tax bracket. I get excited about growing my investments tax free and hope you do too. Just that equals leveraging the resources at your disposal because now money that is ordinarily taxable incurs no taxes when in a Roth IRA.

Self-directed IRA (SD-IRA) accounts strictly are instruments for investments to grow people's retirement accounts. The basics of the self-directed IRA account set-up and several other account mechanics follow, but the focus here is on real estate investments. I provide examples of such investments and how they grow and function within the account.

Said another way, this book is about growing wealth: your wealth. It is about using self-directed IRAs to their best advantage. Become an expert in making such investments in your account, know the basics of the account, and find an excellent and trustworthy custodian to help you navigate IRS rules. The book will show you how you can do that—legally. Always keep in mind that examples are examples only. All investments carry risks and require proper vetting.

A big thank you to the U.S. government for writing that wonderful investment instrument into law in 1997. Read IRS Publication 590, all one hundred and fourteen pages of it, or let your knowledgeable custodian direct you to the most pertinent rules. [v] Some of what Publication 590 contains also appears in this book. [vi]

Let's take advantage of the blessing the U.S. government proffers. Open an SD-IRA, contribute the maximum allowable annual amount, and invest the money. If you are married, maximize the power of SD-IRAs through an account for each spouse. SD-IRAs are also inheritable. Consult with your attorney about the correct way to assign beneficiaries. Briefly, it is best to assign your trust as a beneficiary.

The IRS has several rules for self-directed IRAs that underscore the intent of these accounts. For instance, the accounts disallow one's own home. Their goal is to enable account holders to grow their retirement funds. Our specific focus here is to invest in real estate in these accounts.

Obviously, there are many more IRA rules surrounding SD-IRAs which your custodian, whoever you decide to set your account up with, will be able to explain in great detail. I will only touch on the basics and then showcase real estate investments. Unfortunately, I cannot help you get around the rules of the IRS. I mention this because I've met quite a few creative people who think that purchasing a home for one of their relatives in such an account will help them stay off the radar of the IRS. Personally, I would not chance it. The IRS imposes severe penalties.

It may sound like a downer, but you stand to make tidy returns with an account's intended use. Follow the rules and learn about real estate investments that work in the other chapters. First, though, an overview and discussion about additional reasons for you to continue reading these pages.

Retirement in America in 2021 and beyond

What does retirement look like to you?

The perfect retirement is the one you want to be living. Some of us envision a sunny locale where we listen to the birds or the sound of the surf. Others want to travel the world or to visit museums, to have lunch and dinner with friends and family, to play golf or to paint magnificent pictures.

Whatever your perfect retirement may be, making your scenario a reality takes considerable planning. Without such planning, your retirement reality may be a Social Security check that covers some basics and little more. In that scenario, there may be too many months at the end of the month and too little money to cover it.

Unfortunately, many Americans fall into this category, something which requires them to work longer and to live on (much) less. This sad state of affairs begs for a remedy. To start, it is important to know how much money you might need. Put a number on it. How does that number compare to your current income? Will you need the same amount you are earning today or can you get by with less? If so, how much less?

Consult a retirement income calculator to see how the numbers work out over, say, twenty years of retirement. See the Resources section for retirement and savings calculators.[vii] You may also find them online.

Note that the savings calculator asks at what interest rate you are investing your money . If your current savings generate less than 10% interest, it will be difficult to grow sufficient retirement savings. Unless you already have a sizeable sum in your account.

Many company retirement plans generate much less growth than that. Some of my friends and acquaintances hardly ever look at their plan balances for this reason. It is just too discouraging. Now, if you have such a balance, however paltry, to look at, count your lucky stars.

Some 33% of Americans have no retirement funds at all, while of the remaining 77% fall short in their savings. [viii] According to the U.S. Census Bureau, over sixty percent of Americans will depend on Social Security, charity, friends and family for their retirement. Only roughly 5% of American have the means to retire in comfort and style. [ix]

What a scary scenario!

Most of us are vaguely aware of these sad facts. We now even see movies like Nomadland that show us this reality. When movies such as this one hit the mainstream, they are testament that the problem exists. And it is vexing not to know what to do about the situation. Living in a van is hardly a perfect or a long-term solution.

Yet, many of us continue to *invest in stocks, bonds and mutual funds without realizing that [our portfolios] will never grow large enough to support the over 50 million hopefuls who continue to send their monthly retirement savings to Wall Street. Talk about risky behavior!*[x]

Compound this state of affairs with other components that affect retirement and are beyond our control. These include health care costs, inflation, and stock market fluctuations. What I just described in its simplest form is a recipe for disaster. The good news, however, is that retirement planning with an SD-IRA offers such upside that we must do all we can to use this instrument. That is one big factor we can control, rather than worry about those outside our control.

How well are your retirement investments doing?

To progress to our retirement dreams, we must understand our current situation as regards retirement. Congratulations if you regularly check in to find out your account balances. You are in the minority.

Many people are clueless about the balance of their retirement accounts. Perhaps they dread the numbers and descend into depression because their account nets low returns. Are you among those who do not know your balance? Please see the numbers now.

Investors have no control over stocks, bonds, or mutual funds because all they are doing is directing money into a fund or stock or bond. Markets then drive stocks up or down. Investors cannot control what happens to these investments. Put another way, while you could call up the CEO of the company of the stock you own and say you would like them to improve their performance, it is unlikely that the company pays you any heed.

If, for example, a person with such an IRA account at any brokerage firms such as Schwab, Bank of America, TD Ameritrade, or E-Trade were to call their broker, they would be told that they have a self-directed IRA. Hmm. Why is that? These pages contain the answer to that question.

The good news is that more and more people like yourself are learning about investing your retirement dollars into real estate and other alternative investments through specialty IRAs, which require entirely different custodians than do regular brokerage IRAs. These accounts counts open up opportunities previously unknown to average investors.

For retirement planning tools, you could just search the web and find various calculators. The U.S. Securities and Exchange Commission operates a useful and comprehensive site geared towards investors. The site contains investing and retirement calculators. [xi]

But there is hope. We must focus on what we can control, and it starts with a systemized plan for retirement.

Clearly, how much time we have to build investment funds makes a difference, but it is never too late to start. None of us can hope to enjoy our golden years without thinking and behaving differently than in the past. Self-directed IRAs are excellent planning tools for retirement and making sure that *golden* is the adjective that applies to our final years.

I wrote this book to showcase the ability to invest in real estate via this tool and to inspire you to take action today. Let's talk about why both a plan and a tool like an SD-IRA are indispensable, considering the retirement landscape in America in 2021 and beyond.

Baby Boomers, the large post-World War II generation, were born in 1946 through 1964, a total of 76.4 million Americans. [xii] The Boomers started retiring in 2012. The wave of retiring Boomers continues and by 2030, that entire generation will be eligible for retirement. The only generation after them, approximately as large, is the Millennials, born between 1982 and 2000.

These generations' sheer numbers, besides increased life expectancy, make retirement today and in the future quite different from other generations before them. Shifts in the United States economy and in previously standard social networks demand different approaches to retirement. It is self-made retirement, accounting and being accountable for one's own fortunes and one's financial standing in life, that mostly drives American retirement.

While some Boomers have sufficient retirement monies, many do not. Yet one effect of the pandemic is that more Boomers want to retire earlier than previously planned. Only 55% of this generation has retirement savings and only 27% of those with savings of $100,000 or more.

That leaves a considerable shortfall both for the group with some savings and for those with no savings at all. The numbers suggest trouble and old-age poverty for huge numbers of Boomers. Scary, and no testament to American society, a society with barebones and disappearing social networks.

Social Security will fall short and, even if it delivers, it was neither conceived nor intended to be a replacement for traditional pensions. Anybody who worked the required number of years and who paid into the system will receive benefits. That means the system is egalitarian and pays out to rich and poor alike, commensurate with the entitled parties' contribution. Aside from this, anticipate Social Security benefit reductions as early as 2033.

Social security benefits may not cover much by the time retirement arrives. The system was never intended to fund people's retirement. Social security offers supplementary income only to most Americans. It always did, and the program never intended to fund the bulk of American retirement.

Still, a large percentage of Americans depend on these disappearing benefits. The situation is dire and scary, unless we take matters into our own hands and start planning for retirement in new ways. Counting on social security benefits alone promises a small life.

And will future generations even receive social security benefits? This is particularly concerning now since only a lucky few Americans, mostly government employees, receive pensions in today's political and economic climate.

Even more interesting is that many financial advisors predict retirees will need about 70% of their pre-retirement earnings to maintain a comfortable pre-retirement standard of living. Social security retirement benefits will only replace about 40% of those earning. Without a doubt, other sources of income such as pensions, savings or investments are essential, now more than ever before.

If you're interested in a background story about how retirement in America has changed since at least the 1980s, read Forbes magazine's article in 2018 titled *Where Did All the Pensions Go?*[xiii] The article delineates what happened to retirement monies in America and how Americans are left to their own devices to figure out their retirement. It also points out a few other things about the political background and interests of this development.

Interesting reading, for sure, but at best also a mixed bag for Americans, many of whom struggle with the new economy. Many make ends meet with two or three jobs, a combination of gigs or one old-fashioned job supplemented by a gig. Many have no benefits and save little.[xiv] The Covid-19 pandemic inspired Americans to save more, according to a Time/Next Advisor article.[xv]

While that is good news, it accounts for certain segments of the population because the pandemic caused huge unemployment and the long-term effects are unknown. Although state economies recently opened up, they continue their rebound in some areas while undergoing tremendous shifts in others.

The ramifications of the foregoing brief discussion are that many of us know little or nothing about growing our own retirement funds. How many of us will retire, given this state of affairs? I sincerely hope that you and I are among them, and the thrust of the book is to inspire you to invest in real estate via an SD-IRA to facilitate this.

Many of us have encountered someone with insufficient retirement dollars. It's often a sad affair. As I mentioned in the introduction, retirees who cannot retire because they still need the income from a job, live existences unlike their cohorts in most developed countries who enjoy their lives. They might actually enjoy their lives by traveling, spending time with family, playing golf or bridge, or a slew of other things. If you would rather belong to those who can choose how to spend their last years, then read on about savvy financial planning for your nest egg via an SD-IRA.

Let's focus on how to sail into retirement with full coffers and enjoy it. The aim is neither to count on vanishing pensions nor on uncertain social security benefits or on both. We take the lead by building our own retirement funds with assets that outperform inflation in an SD-IRA. Then, if either pension or social security benefits come our way, they embellish and crown our retirement portfolios. If they do not, we are still in good shape.

As pensions disappeared for many Americans, 401 (k) plan proponents advertised those plans as the solution. Yet the results 401(k) produced were poor for most Americans. During the Recession of 2008, also known as the Great Recession, many Americans found themselves financially diminished or wiped out. Unfortunately, I counted among them, falling prey to a sophisticated out-of-state scheme.

The long recovery that followed and with new demographic, economic and social shifts during the second decade of the 21st century, other approaches and investment vehicles became necessary. As in any time of immense change on almost all levels, novel approaches, opportunism (perhaps the ultimate form of individualism) and even scams often seamlessly fit together.

This remained true after the events of 2008 and 2009. I will address this in more detail in two other chapters in the book: the one on doing one's homework and the one about the dark side of investments.

All that said, SD-IRAs hold immense appeal in the dismal retirement landscape. Plus, they help investors become more literate about finances without playing the stock market. It is perfectly fine, of course, if you like or love the stock market. You might just wish to add real estate investment options to your retirement portfolio.

But not so fast. Most recipients of Social Security scrape by and do nothing more. The government is smart and bases the system on actuarial tables to pay out the least amounts possible or nothing at all, if the recipient dies before the start of drawing the benefits. In addition, it is far from certain whether there will be sufficient funds for eligible recipients.

More probably, the government will either make substantial changes or implement cuts to the program. So far, that has not happened because the Boomers are an influential generation which fights against such measures. However, it is almost certain that the same scenarios will apply to the generations coming after the Boomers.

A pretty bleak picture, unless several things happen. The first of them is better—much better—financial education that includes retirement calculus. Often even MBAs learned nothing of the sort in school and instead learned what I call the MBA business: one which sells services and products reliant on their expertise versus educating the client.

Please know that I respect and appreciate your expertise. I also know that those MBAs working for a large company and corporation support and drive that business' goals. Might there be a sweet spot between sheer profits and serving so many Americans who need better financial information and guidance? I believe the answer is yes.

More socially and environmentally conscious investing is another component we need to address. Although the topic is beyond this book, shifting American demographics show that our society is becoming a renter's nation. Slews of articles and opinion pieces attest to the shift away from the American Dream, a dream once attainable to average Americans.[xvi] [xvii] [xviii]

Though the mythology of the American Dream still pervades the American consciousness, fewer Americans attain its fulfillment. This is true throughout many parts of the country, not just in the most expensive cities. Unsurprisingly, big-time investors with deep pockets are culpable. This affects at least some real estate investing for ordinary Americans who want to retire well and who want to grow wealth. Stay tuned for more on this subject.

Let's return to the larger topic of retirement in the United States in the twenty-first century. When pensions went away—with the exception predominantly of those employed in the government and academic sectors most Americans had to fend for themselves regarding their retirement.

Companies and corporations lobbied for disappearing pensions. They got what they wanted. Their employees, however long-term they may have been, had to work for less with fewer benefits and assume responsibility for their retirement. These trends and developments coincided with being woefully un- or undereducated in the world of finance and with the rise of 401(k)s. The latter is an employer-sponsored retirement contribution plans.

Employers, not employees, administer these plans and charge fees to do so. Employees choose from the investment options their employers offer. Over the years, 401(k)s delivered almost flat results. They barely keep up with inflation. Yet, close to $4 trillion sit in 401(k) accounts.

Perhaps you have a 401(k) and like many such account holders, barely glance at the account statements because they are discouraging to you? If so, you are not alone.

All that said, most of America's $35 trillion retirement market remains invested in stocks, bonds and mutual funds. These Wall Street investments afford investors little or no control over their investments, unless the investors have a lot of money in the market already and can employ more risky strategies, approved by their brokers, such as futures, options, trading on margin, and short selling positions.

Such advanced strategies also involve time commitment and watching the markets and their movements like hawks. I'll stop here as this book is about real estate investing versus Wall Street investing. We'll get back to why brokerage houses like to tell consumers that their IRA's through them are self-directed in a few moments.

For now, many investors put their money in stock, bonds and mutual funds because they are unaware of alternatives. Many of these same investors are also unhappy with their returns but leave their money in them because they do not know any better. And frankly, that is not entirely their fault because the information about self-directed IRAs has only recently found distribution circuits.

Differences between IRAs

Self-directed IRA accounts come in two flavors: a traditional IRA or a Roth IRA. You can have both a traditional IRA and an SD-IRA, if you wish. Perhaps you already have a traditional IRA which holds a sizeable sum of money and investments. If you were to convert that account into a Roth IRA by instructing your custodian or brokerage house to facilitate this, taxes on that money would become due. Often brokerage houses and custodians will hold back those funds.

To weigh whether converting your traditional IRA to a Roth IRA is worthwhile, ask yourself how the cost of the conversion compares to potential tax savings (because you will be in a lower tax bracket). To assess this further, establish what tax bracket you are in now and what tax bracket applies to you when you retire.

The conversion might also in fact bump you into a higher tax bracket. That's something to know beforehand. There are other questions, of course, and a knowledgeable CPA can guide you through the questions to find the facts and align them with your answers.

One important question might be this one: if you were to convert your traditional account to a self-directed account, would you use it or would it just sit there? The answer to that should inform your decision. After all, an account established hardly equals an account in use and growing.

In that case, you may continue to keep a Traditional IRA or do a partial conversion to lessen the tax amount. From that point forward, you might open an SD-IRA and start funding that account with your annual contributions.

Yes, you can have both accounts, but you can only contribute to your normal annual total. If you choose to add the annual contribution to your new self-directed account, the other traditional account will receive no new funds. Or you can decide to split the amounts that total the full annual contribution among the accounts. The IRS assesses a 6% penalty for contributing more than the allowed limit.

As you know, contributions to a traditional IRA happen with pre-tax dollars. A traditional IRA allows you to deduct allowable annual contributions from your taxes. Any investment in a traditional IRA defers taxes on your investment and its growth until a distribution occurs.

At distribution, you owe taxes, usually in the tax bracket you are in. Most people count on their tax bracket being lower when they retire than it would have been during their working lives. Nevertheless, if your investment has grown substantially—the dream and wish of any investor—, the resulting tax bill can be just as substantial.

The good news is that another kind of IRA, one with more benefits to investors whose nest egg grows sizable, came into existence in 1997.

Known as the Roth IRA, named after Senate Finance Committee Chairman William Roth Jr. (R-DE), the account allows contributions with after-tax dollars. A Roth IRA account holder cannot deduct contributions on tax returns, but it allows account owners never to pay taxes on either the money or investments in the account. This is powerful when account growth is healthy and exceeds expectations.

You may now glean the power of investing in real estate, which can exponentially grow accounts when investing in real estate in a self-directed Roth IRA. For this reason, I will focus on Roth IRA real estate investing throughout this book.

To give you a better idea about the difference in investment totals in a traditional and a Roth IRA, consider the following charts.

Traditional Roth

Traditional IRA Returns after 25 Years

$25,000 Initial Investment at 12% and at 15%

——— At 12%   ——— At 15%

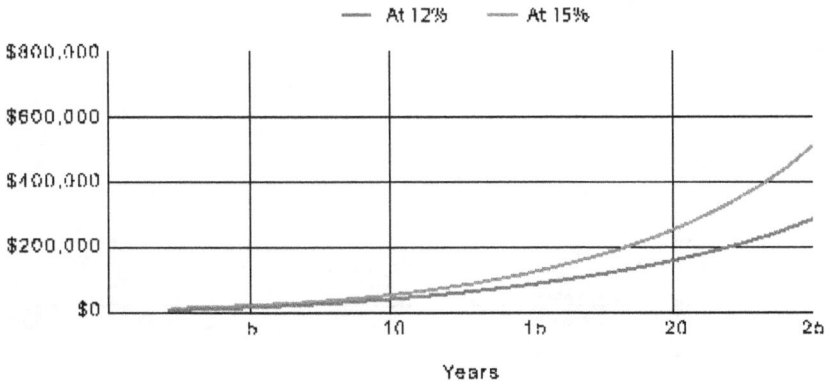

Compared to the same investment growth in a Roth IRA
Roth IRA Initial $25,000 Investment
Tax Free Growth at 12% and at 15% over 25 Years

— At 12%   — At 15%

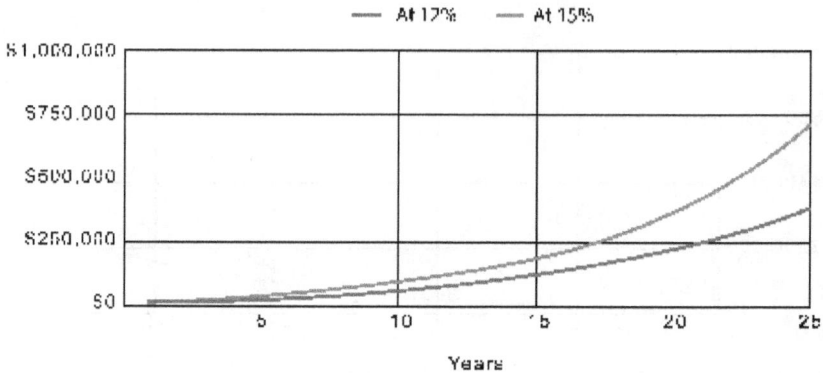

[xix]

The foregoing graphs attest to the power self-directed IRA investment holds. They show the specific returns you choose to invest in for any allowable asset. Note that real estate investments can give higher returns than these. Also, understand that account and asset fees and expenses may alter return percentages. You may wish to aim for a certain return percentage, then plan how to achieve it.

Never forget to include how inflation affects your portfolio. The official rate of inflation as of July 2021 stands at 5.1%. Whatever investment you make should generate a rate of return that stays ahead of inflation. What is the sweet spot that makes this possible? Current advice on this is that it takes anywhere from 4% to 6%. That estimate is rather low. A minimum of 9% to 15% is a better gage.

As you build your portfolio, you find that some instruments return lower percentages and others higher ones. That's okay, especially when portfolio diversification is at play. For example, the portfolio might hold a note that returns 9%, another that returns 12%, and a property bought outright, that returns 7% through the rental income it generates. A seven percent return on a rental property may sound low, but the property is likely to sell at an appreciated value. The portfolio then nets the appreciation amount. You get the idea.

On to your next consideration for understanding and using your SD-IRA account to your advantage. Figure out how long it will take to double your account value when investing with a 10%, 15%, and 20% return. Ask yourself how much effort it will take to invest to net these returns. Though high return percentage assets are seductive, they often represent higher risk levels. If you are a conservative investor, going after high return percentages may run contrary to your nature and comfort level.

Rigorously assess which type of investor you are, and which risk level is right for you. Ask how much money you can afford to lose, if any. Besides this, your time horizon also makes a difference in your choices. Someone two decades away from retirement usually has a different idea and strategy about acceptable investments than someone who is about to retire. Find investing risk assessments online or complete one your broker or custodian offers. Of course, some brokers and custodians offer these investor profiles to sell consulting and advisor services.

Depending on your answers, certain asset classes will be more appropriate than others. How do you find real estate investments that align with the returns you are seeking at the risk level with which you are comfortable? We analyze the various options, and you might well get additional ideas. Evaluate them, then choose wisely. That way, you will mitigate risk when investing in real estate.

The great news happens when you invest much of the money in your self-directed IRA into investments with higher return rates (as discussed above) AND do real estate deals in that same account. Ordinarily, exponential growth is the result. And it might happen faster than you think possible.

In traditional and Roth IRAs and 401(k) plans with brokerage houses versus with self-directed IRA custodians, the money often sits in mutual funds, stocks or bonds. Here, investors have NO control over any of the assets, other than buying or selling them.

You may have a 401(k) plan, a traditional or Roth IRA, a 403(b) plan, or any other plan that helps you save for retirement. What you may not yet have is a self-directed IRA, which can either be a traditional or a Roth IRA. By the way, all IRA accounts are FDIC-insured for up to $250,000.[xx]

I hope I convinced you to open such an account and use it?

Chapter 2: The Nitty Gritty

$$\Omega$$

It is not so much that we are too bold to endure rules; it is rather that we are too timid to endure responsibilities.

- G.K. Chesterton

Rules and regulations

Many years ago, I attended a boarding high school in Germany, run by state employees. The state chose an old Franciscan convent from the 17th century as the school's site. All students there were boarders who had to abide by stringent rules, enforced by the spartan and cold headmistress.

My roommate and I were creative types who disliked many of the rules, including the one that required silence during certain hours. We were teenagers and used to expressing ourselves. The school shunned that as well and within six months of our attendance there, we were on the headmistress' radar and summoned for punitive meetings.

Never ones to let that stand, we founded the school's paper and wrote articles about the rules and their consequences, pointing out how ridiculous they were. This gained us respect and admiration from fellow students but loathing from the administration. Though we had a fun run with this endeavor, you can probably guess who prevailed in the end.

Breaking IRS rules is no different. While all rules are breakable, it is a bad idea to skirt SD-IRA rules. The consequences of breaking the SD-IRA rules are severe. Evaluate them up front and you are likely to find that not adhering to them carries little to no value and can wipe out your nest egg. This is true even if the chances of being discovered are slim. Stay clear of becoming an IRS poster child example of unacceptable behavior.

Your custodian knows the SD-IRA rules and is a wonderful resource to help you stay compliant. The custodian should possess the ability and knowledge to discuss and to help educate you on prohibited transaction rules, allowed IRA assets, and obvious red flags. This is the case even though the custodian does not dispense investment advice and the ultimate responsibility to comply with IRS rules lies with you.

Sure, there are people who break the rules, but if the IRS catches them, the consequences are severe. Adhere to the rules. Your custodian will let you know if you are straying, but the ultimate responsibility to stay on the right side of the rules is yours. Here, then, are the rules that govern these accounts.

Contribution Limits

Contribution limits to traditional and Roth IRAs for 2021 follow. Contribution limits periodically change, so always confirm this information with your custodian.

Consult the table below for contribution limits to traditional and Roth IRAs. An additional component is that there are no income limits for traditional IRAs that stipulate the ability to contribute. However, income limits apply for Roth IRAs for contribution purposes. – The table below applies to both accounts when they qualify. For traditional IRAs, any of these amounts are taxable in the applicable tax bracket at the time of distribution, while this money grows tax-free in Roth IRAs.

Year	Annual Contribution	ROI 10%	Total	15%	Total	20%	Total
	$6,000						
1		$600	$6,600	$900	$6,900	$1,200	$7,200
2		$660	$7,260	$1,035	$7,935	$1,440	$8,640
3		$726	$7,986	$1,190	$9,125	$1,728	$10,368
4		$799	$8,785	$1,369	$10,494	$2,074	$12,442
5		$878	$9,663	$1,574	$12,068	$2,488	$14,930
6		$966	$10,629	$1,810	$13,878	$2,986	$17,916
7		$1,063	$11,692	$2,082	$15,960	$3,583	$21,499
8		$1,169	$12,862	$2,394	$18,354	$4,300	$25,799
9		$1,286	$14,148	$2,753	$21,107	$5,160	$30,959
10		$1,415	$15,562	$3,166	$24,273	$6,192	$37,150
11		$1,556	$17,119	$3,641	$27,914	$7,430	$44,581
12		$1,712	$18,831	$4,187	$32,102	$8,916	$53,497
13		$1,883	$20,714	$4,815	$36,917	$10,699	$64,196
14		$2,071	$22,785	$5,538	$42,454	$12,839	$77,035
15		$2,278	$25,063	$6,368	$48,822	$15,407	$92,442

Note that this contribution table assumes an annual maximum contribution of $6000 and shows its cumulative growth over fifteen years.

2021 Traditional IRA Deduction Limits

You can only deduct contributions to traditional IRAs on your taxes. Roth IRA contributions come from after-tax dollars. Assuming you hold a traditional IRA, contributions deductions in full apply if you and your spouse don't have a 401(k) or some other retirement plan at work. If a plan covers either you or your spouse at work, a reduced deduction may result. Such a plan may even eliminate the deduction. Here's the full rundown of IRA deduction limits for 2021: [xxi] [xxii]

Should you decide to convert a traditional IRA to a Roth IRA, be aware of the rules that apply to these accounts. Rules apply to all taxpayers, of course, but for Roth IRA conversions, important ramifications arise from how high your adjusted gross income is, whether you are single or married, and how you file your taxes.

It may also be helpful for you to know that you may be able to have a Roth IRA, even if you make more than the mandated income threshold. The best way to assess your situation and its complexities is to consult with a knowledgeable CPA or attorney. I will cover more on how to find such a professional in Chapter 5.

Here is an overview of the traditional IRA deduction limits for 2021.

2021 Traditional IRA Deduction Limits

If your filing status is...	Your modified AGI is...	Then you can take...
Single, head of household, qualifying widow(er), married filing jointly or separately and neither spouse is covered by a plan at work	Any amount	Full deduction up to the amount of your contribution limit
Married filing jointly or qualifying widow(er) and you're covered by a plan at work	$105,000 or less	Full deduction up to the amount of your contribution limit
	More than $105,000 but less than $125,000	Partial deduction
	$125,000 or more	No deductions
Married filing jointly and your spouse is covered by a plan at work	$198,000 or less	Full deduction up to the amount of your contribution limit
	More than $198,000 but less than $208,000	Partial deduction
	$208,000 or more	No deductions
Single or head of household and you're covered by a plan at work	$66,000 or less	Full deduction up to the amount of your contribution limit
	More than	Partial deduction

	$66,000 but less than $76,000	
	$76,000 or more	No deductions
Married filing separately and either spouse is covered by a plan at work	Less than $10,000	Partial deduction
	$10,000 or more	No deductions

Unlike Roth IRAs, there are no income limits for contributing to traditional IRAs. And you can deduct your contributions in full if you and your spouse don't have a 401(k) or some other retirement plan at work.

If either one of you is covered by a plan at work, however, the deduction may be reduced or eliminated. Here's the full rundown of the IRA deduction limits for 2021:[1][i2]

---

1. https://mail.google.com/mail/u/0/#m_-2156215483557047242__edn1

2. https://mail.google.com/mail/u/0/#m_-2156215483557047242__edn1

Distributions

Eventually, you will take distributions from an SD-IRA, most likely at retirement. Here is the most important information for our purposes.

Distributions are complex. The 2019 SECURES Act re-applies the required minimum distributions under the new rules. Planning for distributions under the rules is a must. As we focus on setting up SD-IRAs and growing them through real estate investments, no further discussion about the ins and outs of distributions follows. Refer to the Resources section for additional sources about them.

Roth IRAs are more flexible for distributions. While traditional IRAs require the account holder to take minimum distributions at age seventy and a half (70 ½), Roth IRAs allow for continued tax-free growth past that age. Obviously, that only applies to those account holders who do not need that income then.

You can start taking tax-free contributions from your Roth IRA once your account meets the 5-year test, which stipulates that the account must have been in place for 5 years after the first year you received regular contributions. In addition, you must meet the following conditions:

> You must be over 59 ½ years of age.
> You have become disabled.
> You are using up to $10,000 from the account to buy your first home.
> Funds go to your beneficiary after you die.

Other circumstances that allow you to take out early withdrawal funds without a penalty exist, but I do not address them here. You could, however, use your IRA funds to make loans to non-disqualified relatives or friends. If so, create a paper trail. Document the agreement and payments in writing to make it official and easier for you. Always practice caution with loans to such parties.

SD-IRA is inheritable. For a Roth IRA, that means that beneficiaries inherit the account tax-free, so long as the 5-year rule applies. If the account is less than five years old when the account holder dies, the beneficiary must withdraw a minimum amount out for five years and pay taxes on that amount. After that time, all income is tax free.

Disqualified parties

The law stipulates that SD-IRAs act to help and stimulate Americans to save for their retirement. It also anticipated that creative individuals would build wealth networks. This is anathema to the spirit of the law and SD-IRA rules and therefore centers on qualified parties. While the SD-IRA benefits your nest egg, it does not allow transactions that divert profits, payments and loans to yourself or your linear family members. You, your family, and your relatives constitute disqualified parties.

Further, the IRS considers it self-dealing when you engage in prohibited transactions. The IRS deals harshly with self-dealing. Know the rules. Your custodian is also here to help with this, but the ultimate responsibility is yours.

SD-IRA account holders, like almost all human beings, get creative when going after what they want. Some buy property from their parents or other disqualified parties. Others buy vacation homes which they use, if only for a few days or weeks a year. The IRS prohibits these transactions. Stay clear of them.

UDFI and UBIT

Loans are allowable in SD-IRA accounts, but such loans trigger Unrelated Debt Finance Income (UDFI) tax and require filing Form 990-T. UDFI applies to accounts with assets that have debt-financing on them. That happens either when buying a property with a loan, in this case non-recourse, or with "subject to" deals, which I do not cover in this book. The UDFI tax applies to the percentage of the asset's income financed by debt.

Say you decide to purchase a rental property for $150,000, put $50,000 of your own money into the deal and take out a loan for the remaining $100,000. The percentage of debt here is 66%. Therefore, sixty-six percent of the asset's income is subject to UDFI taxes. Consult your non-recourse lender or your CPA for further details.

One way to avoid UDFI taxes is to pay off the debt at least 12 months before selling the asset. Another option might be via an SD-IRA LLC, but for this option, legal fine points apply and only an excellent attorney who understands these special LLCs can dissect this further.

Yet another way to avoid this tax is through Joint Ventures (JVs). In that case, the account holder and another investor become equity partners and leverage resources and expertise. Neither debt nor UDFI result in JVs. Other considerations apply to JV arrangements, as structuring them correctly is quite important. Consult the right professionals to assess which options are best for your account.

Of course, many SD-IRA account holders have no loans in their accounts, which means UDFI does not apply to their SD-IRA. However, they might engender Unrelated Business Taxable Income (UBITs) for other reasons, some of which lie within gray zones and are open to interpretation.

For example, if you buy real estate and then sell it immediately or hold it for less than a year, the IRS might consider you a flipper (a business) and ask you to pay taxes. You must pay these business-related taxes out of your SD-IRA. You cannot pay them via your personal or business accounts. If this happens, your IRA custodian will guide you through the event and ask you to file Form 990-T.

Determination of whether you are a flipper lies with the IRS, which often considers over one or two such transactions within a short time a business. Hence, the IRS mandates taxes in those cases. While contesting such IRS determinations is possible, it is paperwork and time-intensive, and therefore better to circumvent this altogether. I hope you agree.

Your custodian has reporting duties to the IRS. Still, little documentation about how many SD-IRA accounts get caught flipping over one or two properties a year exists. You could take the risk, of course, but why? In the name of making more money, or to prove you can do it, or to buck the system? At the very least, consult and strategize with your CPA and attorney to achieve the best outcome where UBIT can be assessed.

There are other instances when UBIT applies, for example when operating a business within the SD-IRA. [xxiii] Investigate owning a business in an SD-IRA and all the rules that govern such an investment. This book only deals with owning real estate in these specialty accounts.

Prohibited SD-IRA Assets and Transactions

Prohibited asset classes and transactions include:

➤ Your own home.

➤ Loans to yourself.

➤ Properties in which you have a controlling interest.

➤ Rental properties you own in your name, not the IRAs.

> Buy or sell properties to or from yourself or disqualified parties.

> Indirect benefits, such as renting a space in a property your SD-IRA owns. The same applies to vacation homes you own in your SD-IRA. You cannot take a vacation there or stay in the property for other purposes.

> You cannot pay yourself income from your SD-IRA. All income must flow back into the account.

> Your SD-IRA must pay all expenses for assets inside the account.

> Insurance.

> Collectibles like artworks, stamps, rugs, etc.

> Note that some U.S. coins are allowed investments.

Now a short list of prohibited transactions follows. Please remember that prohibited transactions and disqualified parties often intersect. Here is the list.

1. Owning your home in your SD-IRA. I know you'd like to put your home into the account, but you cannot.
2. Properties in which you have a controlling interest.
3. property in your account that belongs to a prohibited (disqualified)

party. No, no, no.

4. Collectibles, such as antiques, artwork, gems and stamps.
5. Drugs or alcohol.
6. Precious metals, except for some US coins.

Penalties for prohibited transactions

What are the consequences of engaging in prohibited transactions in your SD-IRA?

The IRS imposes severe penalties on prohibited transactions and dealings and may even wipe out the entire account in question. Now, you may ask how the IRS would know about this.

Well, they can audit your account. It happens, though no one knows how often. Or the SD-IRA custodian discovers a prohibited transaction and distributes the account. The custodian does so by filing a 1099-R. Or the SD-IRA account holder declares bankruptcy, or a creditor or bankruptcy trustee attempts to remove the account's creditor protections. Other legal fine prints apply and some excellent books that cover the topic in depth appear in the bibliography.

Even if the risk of getting caught is slim, why chance it? In a word, it's just not worth it.

Let's move on to what triggers penalties.

- Self-dealing.
  - Self-dealing refers to any asset over which you have control. Involvement in a transaction in which family or relatives are parties or one in which you put a property that you own in your own name versus in your IRA account are red flags. So are you making yourself or a family member the property manager for your IRA-held property and paying a salary? Or loaning money to yourself. Other scenarios exist, but you get the idea.
- Investing in excluded assets.
  - It's easy enough to read the list of ineligible assets. Your custodian might also advise you on this when you request investing in such an asset.
- Loaning yourself money from your IRA.
- Using your IRA as security for a loan.
- Completing services for IRA-held properties yourself and paying

yourself to do so.
  ◦ This falls under self-dealing.

For example, if your SD-IRA holds a vacation rental, neither you nor your family can use the vacation home, not even for a day. The same applies to owning an office building in your SD-IRA. Neither you nor your family can use an office or other space in that building. Or if you own land in the SD-IRA, you or your family cannot farm or otherwise use this land.

You might get more creative and loan money to a disqualified party, like your children or other relatives. The IRS prohibits this and will tax you a hefty 15% on the disqualified transaction amount. As if that were not enough, the IRS expects you to correct the prohibited transaction. Your custodian can help do that, but it is costly and a hassle.

In case the transaction remains as is, meaning you do not correct it, the IRS will levy a 100% additional tax. Additionally, the IRS may decide to dissolve your account, which results in all the account assets becoming distributions at fair market value on the first day of the year. When that happens, you will have a taxable event which becomes part of your taxes, should the account value exceeds its basis.

Ouch. What Draconian and painful scenarios!

If your SD-IRA ceases to exist, you can no longer invest tax-free. Even if it still exists, the penalties might wipe you out, so there is no good reason to take the risk. You get the idea.

Hopefully, this deters you from doing something untoward in the name of a quick profit. Take it as a big warning. Instead, get wealthy the legal way. Your SD-IRA facilitates just that, and this book shows you how.

Time, money, expertise

Clients sometimes ask me how much time, money and expertise investing in real estate through a self-directed IRA requires. Answers to this question vary and often depend on your specific situation. It helps us to understand the important basics and rules of SD-IRAs—see next section.

While time and expertise can supercharge your portfolio, they are not always necessary. As for the money, you will need as little as the amount your custodian requires to keep the account in good standing. If you wish to buy an investment outright, your account must have sufficient funds for the transaction, any other costs associated with it, and funds to maintain your account. When I said that a sizeable amount of funds in the account are sometimes unnecessary, I meant that your risk tolerance and your ability to leverage what you have in either money, time, expertise and sheer brain power are specific to you.

Now, you may wonder how to get rich with an SD-IRA when you have no obligation to contribute annually to the account. First, I encourage you to make your annual contribution to the fullest extent possible because that will help you grow consistently and faster. If you contribute that money to a Roth IRA, it grows tax free. Here's what that looks like over time:

Year Annual Contribution ROI

Year	Annual Contribution	10%	Total	15%	Total	20%	Total
	$6,000						
1		$600	$6,600	$900	$6,900	$1,200	$7,200
2		$660	$7,260	$1,035	$7,935	$1,440	$8,640
3		$726	$7,986	$1,190	$9,125	$1,728	$10,368
4		$799	$8,785	$1,369	$10,494	$2,074	$12,442
5		$878	$9,663	$1,574	$12,068	$2,488	$14,930
6		$966	$10,629	$1,810	$13,878	$2,986	$17,916
7		$1,063	$11,692	$2,082	$15,960	$3,583	$21,499
8		$1,169	$12,862	$2,394	$18,354	$4,300	$25,799
9		$1,286	$14,148	$2,753	$21,107	$5,160	$30,959
10		$1,415	$15,562	$3,166	$24,273	$6,192	$37,150
11		$1,556	$17,119	$3,641	$27,914	$7,430	$44,581
12		$1,712	$18,831	$4,187	$32,102	$8,916	$53,497
13		$1,883	$20,714	$4,815	$36,917	$10,699	$64,196
14		$2,071	$22,785	$5,538	$42,454	$12,839	$77,035
15		$2,278	$25,063	$6,368	$48,822	$15,407	$92,442

But even if your account only has a small amount of cash in it, you will achieve "a high rate of return by leveraging your brain, not your money." These are the words of Ron LeGrand, a real estate guru who is an expert in seller financing and option contracts. I am not and stay away from them for that reason.

Leveraging your brain, however, is essential in any kind of investing.

Chapter 3: The Pros of SD-IRAs

Ω

As we enjoy great advantages from the inventions of others, we should be glad of an opportunity to serve others by any invention of ours, and this we should do freely and generously.
- Benjamin Franklin

Beyond Wall Street investments

Opportunities and ferreting out advantages inspire and propel you to results and success. SD-IRAs offer advantages and allow account holders to invest in alternative investments, investments unavailable in other accounts. When I first learned about this government-approved vehicle, it appeared too good to be true. Ever the researcher, a lot of reading and analyzing followed. My conclusion about this powerful tool is that its advantages (pros) outweigh its disadvantages (cons).

The pros of SD-IRAs mostly concern the investor's ability to grow their accounts with much bigger returns than most other available investment vehicles. The reasons for this include alternative investment availability, more control over the investments, diversification, and the creation of tax wealth. A closer look at them follows in this chapter.

Control over your investments

Perhaps you, like me, know someone who displays anal tendencies, perhaps about their appearance, orderliness in their surroundings, or telling others to do things a certain way. Usually, such a person allows for no other possibilities and insists it's their way or the highway. Perhaps you yourself need to do this to feel safe. In fact, we all have areas in our lives that look like this, yet there is a fine line between good decision making and demands that self-defeat.

When investing in anything, the issue of control rears its head, often as having little or no control. While many factors influence investment performance and some of these factors, like market fluctuations and inflation, remain out of our control, SD-IRAs afford much more control of the investments in an account. For example, an SD-IRA real estate investor can rent, improve, develop, or otherwise benefit from the real estate assets in the account.

SD-IRA regulations require that account holders make all decisions related to their account and the investments in it. The custodian acts in strict accord with account holders' directions. The custodian acts as the facilitator for account holders and while that implies some control over the paperwork, you can even circumvent much of it with a checkbook LLC tied to your SD-IRA.

An instructive example of what investors can and can't control from my own SD-IRA investing follows. My first SD-IRA real estate investment occurred in 2005. It was the height of the market and appeared set to continue in this vein. Yet everything in the portfolio went straight into the crash of 2007. All the options to exit the assets disappeared: selling them was near impossible, the renters in them defaulted, and redeveloping them was no option.

The *if only I had more control syndrome* permeated my thoughts until a review of my stock portfolio jolted me into a fresh perspective. Compared to the stock portfolio, the investments in the SD-IRA account afforded me much more control. The unfortunate reality was that I could not control the markets and the economy. I had no crystal ball but lucky for me, I limped away from the experience a couple of years later.

This investment failure held huge lessons. For one, it honed my decision-making process and imposed more stringent investment criteria. For another, it emphasized the importance of sufficient reserves in the account. The reason I am telling you this is to make better real estate investment decisions in your account and to understand what lies in your control and what does not.

In summary, the things I could not control led to better decision-making. Life does not hold any guarantees and SD-IRA investments are no exceptions, though they come as close to a guarantee as I can imagine. Taking control of an SD-IRA offers a great way to shape one's destiny, something that the American Dream and its mythology imply. Most real estate asset classes produce much better returns than stocks, bonds and mutual funds. They are also less volatile than the stock market.

Real Estate Investments

Real estate captures the imagination of a large swath of investors and for good reason. Mark Twain's famous saying *buy land, they don't make it anymore* extends to everything that land holds or could hold. Real estate investments often generate considerably higher returns than many other investments, given you do your homework and continue to learn about the investment category or categories of most interest.

Naturally, the disclaimer of *past performance is no guarantee of future results* applies to all investments. The examples in this book provide you with ideas, strategies, and approaches to inspire you to intelligent action. Your own examples will be most instructive and representative once you gain real estate investment experience.

Among the many options in real estate investments, choose what fits your investment objectives, your experience, and your personality. Once you understand the different options, this will be easy. At the moment, here is the list of real estate-specific investment asset classes the IRS allows. Read Chapter 6 for more details about each one.

> Condos
> Single-family homes
> Multi-unit buildings
> Apartment buildings
> Land
> Parking lots
> Self-storage units
> Office and retail properties
> Mortgage notes
> Tax liens and tax deeds

The above list is incomplete. Read the second book in this series, titled *Finding Profitable Deals,* for information about these asset classes and how to find them. The book also details other real estate asset possibilities.

Most of us either own a home or want to own one, so our psyches tie into real estate when connected to one of our survival needs, the need to lay our heads down and to do so safely. This, of course, means that the need for real estate, whether as a single-family home or an apartment, occupies our thoughts. We strive to achieve this security.

Since all of us seek a place to call home, opportunities exist to help others fulfill that need, either as owners or as renters. With that, we can make money, shape lives, and contribute to communities and to society. Although the thrust here is on making money via investments, the other subjects directly tie into it and I believe it a good idea for investors to discern the impact they have on others' lives.

One last mention of real estate investments. They constitute hard assets, which are physical or tangible assets that have intrinsic value. Real estate such as land, houses and other types of buildings belong to the hard asset category. Their value lies in the ability to produce goods and services that often create cash flow. By the way, most real estate notes and tax liens tie to the underlying real estate, which guarantees them. Those are paper investments.

Diversification

One obvious advantage of SD-IRAs is the ability to diversify investments beyond stocks, bonds, mutual funds, and ETFs. Traditional brokerage house investments like these afford investors little control. In those scenarios, investors buy shares at certain prices and hold or option them, then sell them. Market direction drives all these actions. Unlike with real estate investments, investors lack the ability to affect the performance of the companies whose shares they hold.

A few real estate diversification examples include a land investment that its owner can rent, lease, option, sub-divide, or develop. Or a multi-family home where the investor can either rent, renovate or otherwise improve, and eventually sell the property. The investor decides and directly affects profits. While market forces are still in play, the investor's vision and abilities can adapt to them in better ways.

In a retirement account like the SD-IRA, diversification is especially important, one that extends past stocks and bonds. Such diversification allows you to tap into different markets and sectors, and better return potential. Investment choices are manifold, so long as they abide by IRS rules. The ability to invest in real estate in its many forms in your SD-IRA also acts as a hedge against the volatility normal for a stock, bond, and mutual fund portfolio.

Tax-wealth

Unless you are an American billionaire like Jeff Bezos, Bill Gates or Elon Musk, you are likely to pay a fair amount of taxes. Ordinary Americans need all the help they can get to pay fewer taxes and what is better than an instrument the government provides them?

The creation of tax wealth is another major advantage an SD-IRA account passes to account holders. The SD-IRA empowers account holders to create wealth with money ordinarily owed as taxes, whether by deferring taxes on investments in a traditional IRA or growing investment returns tax-free. While I prefer the latter, some investors have valid reasons to use traditional IRAs. Individual circumstances vary and it is of tantamount importance to work with knowledgeable CPAs and attorneys to find the best solution.

In a traditional IRA, you make annual contributions that you can deduct on your income taxes. Your money in a traditional IRA then grows in various ways via the investments of your choice. As distributions begin and continue, you pay taxes on investment returns in the tax bracket you now fall into. Your money grows tax-deferred. A traditional IRA is a tax-advantaged account.

You can also make contributions in a Roth SD-IRA, but the money funding that account is after-tax money. This means you cannot deduct the contribution amount on your taxes. However, because you already paid taxes on these contributions, they now grow tax free. What a boon that is!

Please review the comparison tables in Chapter 1 that show considerable differences in returns in the traditional and Roth SD-IRA accounts.[xxiv]

Ability to set up an LLC

Some SD-IRAs allow for checkbook control. A checkbook IRA is a legal entity and instrument specific to your SD-IRA. This gives you, as the appointed LLC manager, checkbook control over the funds in your account. This control allows you to sign contracts, write checks, and to receive and pay expenses, instead of instructing the custodian to do so. That saves you time and money. No further delays or transaction fees.

Sounds great, right?

Well, you may or may not need checkbook control.

Many potential and new SD-IRA account holders view an IRA LLC and checkbook control as a boon and they are, but many SD-IRAs do not need checkbook control, at least not when starting out with one or two investments. IRA LLCs are powerful once the account grows and if the account holds several investments. Although you incur fees to set-up a Checkbook IRA and annual LLC tax payments in the state in which the LLC operates, custodial fees are much lower when many assets are in the entity. That is because the SD-IRA's only asset is the LLC.

Again, it is better to understand the SD-IRA first and decide on a strategy for it. Do your research to see if your IRA investment strategy requires an LLC or checkbook control. Verify the annual fees or taxes you might get stuck with if you choose an LLC. Depending on the investment and how many, you may not need an LLC.

For example, if your account holds rental real estate or properties that undergo development and renovation, an LLC may offer you some liability protection. While that carries truth, SD-IRAs are instruments that are for your benefit and connected to you. They are not separate entities. That means that you may personally be liable for any action taken in the account. Legal precedents exist and your attorney can divulge the nitty-gritty of how liability works for SD-IRA accounts.

If you decide that a checkbook IRAs is the right instrument for you, please hire a competent attorney. It is highly unlikely that generic LLC documents you find or purchase online will result in properly drafted LLC documents and the correct operating agreement for the entity. These specialty LLCs require the correct language. The correct LLC set-up is an important qualification for the account; if incorrect, the account may owe taxes.

In case you already own an LLC outside your SD-IRA, you cannot use that LLC for this account. You and your legal counsel must create an LLC tailored to the SD-IRA.

Once the LLC documents are in place, the attorney who drafted them will provide a letter of opinion to the SD-IRA custodian. Once complete, funds from the SD-IRA will move into the LLC bank account as per instructions to the custodian. Then the LLC is ready to make investments. All of its investments ought to carry the name of the LLC and must adhere to the disqualified parties and prohibited transaction regulations the IRS stipulates.

Custodians for SD-IRA can file any necessary account paperwork for the account and ensure that the account adheres to IRS regulations. This applies to every transaction in the account. However, when a Checkbook IRA is in place, the custodian no longer approves investment legality. This means that the onus is now on the account holder alone. Protect yourself and your account by getting qualified advice about any transaction's legality.

We are now moving on to the cons of SD-IRAs, most of which deal with regulations and having to deal with a third party, your custodian. Read through the cons and keep in mind that the pros of SD-IRAs trump the next section, but that you must know and understand the information that follows.

Chapter 4: Cons of SD-IRA Investing

Ω

You have to learn the rules of the game, and then you have to play better than anyone else.
- Albert Einstein

Rules permeate our lives and although we often dislike rules and even skirt them, they serve us most times. It seems almost everything has written and unwritten rules: our work, social etiquette, relationships, traffic, public and private venues, and the list goes on. As one might expect, the IRS is no exception in issuing red tape to level the playing field and prevent unfair advantages. Even if you rail against them, know them besides your custodian's role. Evaluate the consequences of breaking any of these rules before you invest. That one action will serve you well and you are likely to find that SD-IRAs are worth it despite the rules.

Your custodian helps navigate these waters, so find one who is responsive and knowledgeable. Let's look at what the disadvantages for SD-IRAs are. They follow in no particular order.

Paperwork

IRS regulations require a good amount of paperwork. There is no way around it, but once you are familiar with which forms you need to complete and how to do that, it is a cinch. Some common forms include expense payment requests, representative authorizations, beneficiary authorizations, investment authorizations, and transfer authorizations.

Nowadays custodians have form repositories on their website. Once you log into your account and pull up the forms, simply fill them out and DocuSign them. That way, they will transmit to the custodian right away.

Of course, you can also print out the forms and either mail them or fax them to the custodian if you are more comfortable doing so.

All SD-IRAs rely on paperwork that ensures compliance with IRS rules, regulations, and codes. Your custodian is knowledgeable in this arena and usually has a forms library for your use. If you have questions about these forms, email or call your custodian. Some common forms include expense payment requests, representative authorizations, beneficiary authorizations, investment authorizations, and transfer authorizations.

SD-IRAs require a lot of paperwork, though the good news is that your custodian creates, executes, and records the paperwork. Of course, you still have a part in completing the paperwork. The custodian must also sign off on all contracts.

Oodles of paperwork have drawbacks. For one, using the right forms and correctly filling them out is imperative. The sheer volume of paperwork may also take more time for tasks and transactions to complete. Custodians keep an 8 to 5 business day schedule. They do not work on weekends. Always factor that into your timelines.

That said, if you have an SD-IRA with checkbook control, you will move faster. Checkbook control for your account also saves on fees as custodians charge for almost every piece of paper that crosses their desk. Read more about the differences between IRAs with and without checkbook control in the section with that title.

Fees

As I mentioned earlier, SD-IRA custodians are trust companies and banks from regular brokerages. These companies adhere to certain requirements and their fees are higher for that reason, but they range. Fees add up, so understanding how the custodian charges and for what is quite important. It can spell the difference between wiping out your profits or keeping most of them. Even though custodian fees can be significant, they matter much less when the investor makes high returns. Over the past twenty years, more custodians entered the field, so be sure to compare their services and fees. They vary.

If you opt to establish an SD-IRA-specific LLC, your life will be much easier because it affords you checkbook control. Plus, you can save money by setting up such a LLC. Just remember such a LLC makes the most sense if you have multiple assets in your account because your custodian normally charges asset and transaction fees on every asset and transaction. A LLC minimizes these fees.

Naturally, start-up costs apply when establishing an LLC for this purpose. You must therefore weigh whether such an LLC is helpful to you, especially if your account only contains one or two investments. You will also save on administrative and transaction fees with an SD-IRA-specific LLC. Some custodians offer checkbook control, while others do not. Refer to the section designed for easy custodian comparison to see which ones offer checkbook control.

Checkbook control comes in handy when paying expenses, whether for property taxes or repairs or property management fees. Instead of filling out the custodian's expense request form and waiting for them to carry out your instructions, having a checkbook tied to your SD-IRA account allows you to "cut out" the custodian. That way, you are not at the mercy of the custodian's turnaround times and save on the fees they assess for these individual services.

Use the SD-IRA checkbook for your account only. The IRS will not allow you to write checks from other unrelated accounts. Doing so is self-dealing and spells trouble, but you are smarter than engaging in that, right?

IRS Regulation

Government-backed instruments like the SD-IRAs are subject to regulation. The regulations are complex. That is hardly a surprise, nor that the account must be compliant. Otherwise, the risk that the IRS disqualifies the account is great. Risks include having to pay taxes and penalties immediately upon the IRS deeming the account disqualified.

How to mitigate this risk?

Your SD-IRA custodian will help you navigate the regulations. That is why a knowledgeable custodian is invaluable. You still must do your part and learn the rules and regulations about buying, selling, financing, and managing property in your account. Leverage your custodian's knowledge and expertise while building your own.

Expensive investments

Overall, real estate investments are expensive investments and this truth also applies to real estate assets in your SD-IRA. You may have considerable cash amounts to invest in real estate in the account. Perhaps you rolled over your 401(k) or liquidated stocks and bonds. If so, that would be great, and you may be able to buy the property outright.

Stay with me if your account is smaller. You still have options that might serve you well to grow your real estate portfolio. The possibilities include optioning property, investing in tax liens or notes, and partnering. Or you could secure a non-recourse loan, in which case you would pay taxes on some or all of the income the underlying asset generates. Or you could become a lender to other investors yourself, a private lender, or find such a lender to facilitate a transaction on which this makes sense. I will discuss these options in Chapter 6.

Factor in that you will pay for inspections, appraisals, closing costs, title insurance, renovations, maintenance, taxes, property insurance, property management, and various other fees. Many expenses apply to any property and your account must have sufficient reserves to cover them.

All the factors discussed in this section are drawbacks and only you can decide— along with knowledgeable and trusted professionals— whether the advantages in investing in real estate in your SD-IRA outweigh these. I believe they do in most cases, but please evaluate what is right for you. It's one thing if fear grips you and a completely different situation when you evaluate these puzzle pieces considering your situation.

Undoubtedly, you know that risk is inherent in all investments. Take intelligent risks and never speculate or bend the rules when using an SD-IRA. Do your homework on any investment you consider. I will detail how to do this in the section on due diligence. You are likely to develop your own due diligence process once you complete this important background work several times.

Unrelated debt-financing income

Unrelated debt-financing income or UDFI relates to any property you finance through a debt instrument, such as a loan, in your SD-IRA. A certain amount of the income for that property is taxable.

Maybe you purchase a $100,000 property with $50,000 of your SDIRA funds and $50,000 in debt. This fifty-fifty split means that the portion you financed with debt represents the portion of your net income to which UDFI applies. You annually pay taxes on 50% of your net income on this asset.

However, UDFI is more complex than stated in this simple example. Some exceptions and exclusions might apply to your situation. Consult with your tax professional to understand the UDFI specific to your situation.

Liquidity considerations

When investing in real estate, always consider that property is a more illiquid asset than say stocks or bonds are. Besides that, real estate experiences market fluctuations just like the financial markets. Down and up markets look quite different, especially when buying and selling property.

Therefore, consider what strategy might best work to accomplish your goals. If you are only fixing and flipping properties, market fluctuations can affect what happens to your profits. They might well evaporate in a down market when it seems impossible to move the assets off your books.

Here is a cautionary tale that happened to me.

I bought land some twenty years ago on the promise that the land would appreciate. That seemed true, as it was in an area with considerable and purported development. I paid taxes on this illiquid and undeveloped parcel for several years. Its value stayed fairly constant, and I was fine with that. The parcel sat in my SD-IRA and investing in land is a long game, in most cases. Then the Great Recession hit. Development in the area faltered, hiccupped and fizzled, and values plummeted to a third of what I paid for it.

Well, this situation continued for several years. My investment degraded to a big red ink balance, and I considered myself lucky when finally selling it at a tiny fraction of its original cost. This was not the idea of growing a retirement portfolio, but I learned many valuable lessons from this horrible investment.

The type of property you buy and the market environment have a tremendous impact on the profits you make. I learned that lesson the hard way, but you read my cautionary tale here, absorbing the lesson and hopefully avoiding my mistake.

You will most likely make your own mistakes. Knowing this, leave a financial cushion to help you absorb any you might make. And develop the attitude that mistakes help you grow and become better. Eventually, your investments will flourish.

The 5-Year Waiting Period

Last but not least, the IRS stipulates a 5-year waiting period for Roth SD-IRAs. Whatever does this mean?

Think of the 5-year waiting period as vesting your account. The clock starts to run when you open your account. The 5-year rule stipulates that you must wait at least 5 years after your first contribution to the Roth IRA for any withdrawals to be tax free. (See the rules that apply to withdrawals in that section.)

If the Roth IRA account holder dies before that time, the account's beneficiary must pay taxes on investment growth for the next five years, at which point any account withdrawals become tax free.

A 5-year waiting period also applies to traditional IRAs, but here the rule states that the IRA beneficiaries who are not taking life expectancy payments must withdraw the entire IRA balance by December 31 in the year of the fifth anniversary of the owner's death. For example, if the owner died in 2019, the beneficiary would have to distribute the plan in full by December 31, 2024. The beneficiary is allowed, but not required, to take distributions prior to that date. The 5-year rule never applies if the owner died on or after his or her required beginning date.

The 5-year rule applies to all beneficiaries, whether individuals or trusts, if the IRA account holder died in a year that ended before 2020. If the account owner died in a year that ended after 2019 and the beneficiary is an individual, the 10-year rule applies.

The 10-Year Rule

The 10-year rule stipulates that any IRA beneficiaries who are not taking life expectancy payments must withdraw the entire balance of the IRA by December 31 of the year in which the 10th anniversary of the account holder's death falls. If the account holder died in 2020, the beneficiary must withdraw the entire IRA balance by December 31, 2030. The beneficiary may also take distributions prior to that date.

The beneficiary elects the 10-year rule if the account holder died before reaching his required beginning date. This rule also applies when the beneficiary is a designated beneficiary who is not an eligible designated beneficiary. In that case, it does not matter if the account holder died before reaching his or her required beginning date.

Note that beneficiaries who fail to follow distribution rules are subject to hefty excise taxes on balances left in their accounts after the designated time periods. [xxv]

These rules contain additional details which extend beyond this book. We discuss the rules' basics here so you know they exist. Your attorney and/or custodian will be able to shed more light on them. Please consult with them. You may also start understanding all their details by reading IRS Publication 590[xxvi] and by reading books about self-directed IRAs written by attorneys. Attorneys approach the subject from the legal perspective it deserves. CPAs who understand SD-IRAs and the IRS rules surrounding them can also guide you.

Taxes and SD-IRAs

One of my favorite Bay Area monologists who writes his own material is Josh Kornbluth. He produced a hilarious monologue titled *Love and Taxes* several years ago. In case you want to lighten the subject of tax evasion and other tax snafus a bit, you can now even watch it via subscription or on demand online. But I digress from the last con, which really is a quasi-con.

SD-IRA account holders who are either uninformed or defiant can inflict this one on themselves. In either case, the account holder suddenly owes taxes and penalties, something the SD-IRA account supposedly has nothing to do with in the first place.

So what is going on?

If you read the section on penalties and how they happen, you already know most reasons and triggers that net you a tax bill. A hefty one at that. The following are red flags the IRS moves on:

- Prohibited transactions.
- Operating a business in your account.
- Buying property with debt financing such as *subject to*.
  - Note that *subject to* qualifies as debt financing. Taking out a non-recourse loan from a bona fide lender to finance your property transaction is different.

Read the full list of allowable investments in IRS publication 590. As already mentioned, your custodian will help you stay clear of prohibited assets and transactions. Still, the ultimate responsibility to adhere to the rule's rests with you.

At the risk of sounding like a broken record, SD-IRAs help people grow their retirement funds. Growing one's everyday accessible now wealth is not allowed in these accounts. Nor are speculative investments.

All the rules you just read may turn you off. I understand if you are, but I want to point out that SD-IRAs offer immense benefits. I know of no other investment vehicle other than the Roth SD-IRA that allows for tax-free growth of account gains.

Turning Cons into Pros

Did your eyes glaze over while reading the information in this chapter? Or does the temptation to skip it cross your mind? All these cons may trigger frustration with SD-IRA account rules and regulations in you, but before starting to rail against the government and the IRS, consider that these parameters still allow for growing your retirement funds through profitable investments. You are also unlikely to change the rules that govern SD-IRAs.

The most prudent approach is to know the rules and stay clear of violating them. The good news here is that your custodian and other competent professionals are assisting in SD-IRA account compliance. They can point out anything out of line with the rules and regulations, naturally only if you consult them and run both your investments and investment scenarios by them. Custodians can also deal with SD-IRA paperwork on your behalf.

It only stands to reason that custodian fees are worth their while to keep you on the right side of the law and handle much of the minutiae. Even though custodian fees are high, they should matter little to you when your investments grow more than you ever imagined possible. Furthermore, if you have ordinary brokerage house accounts, fees seem low when they often are not. You just may not see them because the price you pay for the stock, bond, ETF or mutual fund includes them.

Real estate can be expensive investments, but lower price tag options exist and I discussed those in Chapter 6. High or higher price tags should therefore not deter you, especially when doing your homework, as detailed in Chapter 7. Here you make certain that the investment holds commensurate value, and your cash flow with it from the start. Appreciation alone is a poor idea.

In tandem with this, consider that, while real estate lacks the liquidity of stocks and bonds, your SD-IRA should not need to sell property right away. It is, after all, an account to grow your retirement funds. Consider it as on par with a 401(k) or 403(b). Plan on touching the money only when you must take contributions and devise the most beneficial strategy to do so when that time arrives.

Your power with an SD-IRA lies in putting the instrument to work as soon as you can. The rules and regulations are part and parcel of it, so learn them. Do your best to overcome the instinct to defy them.

Chapter 5: How to Find the Right Professionals

Ω

There is no such thing as a self-made man.
You will reach your goals only with the help of others.
— George Shinn

Searches on just about any subject on the internet make a great deal of information gathering possible. A false sense of confidence and a *going-it-alone* mentality can result. It is wonderful to gather information and to assimilate the subject at hand but dispensing with the right team in real estate investing is a big mistake, even if you can do it all yourself. Real estate investing without a competent team is akin to needing a medical procedure and operating on yourself.

You may read other books and articles on real estate investing that claim you can navigate it all on your own. I believe that is foolish, unless you already have a lot of experience or are an accountant, a realtor®, or an attorney. Even then, other complimentary professionals, such as property managers, non-recourse lenders, and inspectors, are vital.

You are likely to dive into the investment seas without a headlamp when going at it alone. Darkness surrounds you there. The right team, however, sheds light and lifts you (and your investments) with each team member's special skills. Together they will help you vet real estate investment opportunities and navigate legal and financial rules and implications.

Finding the right professionals

The team you put together can make or break you. When assembling your team, find a CPA or an attorney who knows about and understands self-directed IRAs. This sounds easy enough. Unfortunately, many CPAs and attorneys do not understand self-directed IRAs. You can find such individuals by searching the internet (a start but unreliable), by growing your network, and by referral from other experienced investors or from custodians. All of those are valid methods, but always vet anyone you hire yourself. Interview them and check references and reviews.

Your team includes the custodian, an attorney, an accountant, a realtor®, and a title officer/company. Calling in other professionals, such as insurance agents, inspectors, contractors and others may also apply. This seems like a tall order and even unnecessary in the era of turnkey, done-for-you real estate investing but you pay for it in the property mark-up anyhow and may learn only the aspects of the property the turnkey seller wants you to know. Even though we live in a disclosure-heavy environment, not all disclosures are equal. Having your own team in place is a must.

If you cannot find professionals knowledgeable about SD-IRAs, you could educate the attorneys, accountants, realtors®, and other professionals by providing them with IRS Code 590 booklet, which relays the pertinent information. A word of caution, though: while educating others is possible, it may prove time- and labor-intensive. Instead of becoming an expert on the ins and outs of SD-IRAs and evangelizing them, focus on your real estate investment course within your own account. It pays much better.

Assemble your team before you need it, so that when a brilliant investment appears you can immediately make a move. Hundreds of investment possibilities will pop up once you seek them, but only one or two or three will be the right ones for you after you vet them. We get into how to do that in Chapter 7.

The custodian

Even with all the rules, SD-IRAs are amazing wealth growth vehicles. The first step in establishing an SD-IRA account is to identify the right custodian. The custodian you choose will help you mitigate many of the cons discussed in chapter 4. Your custodian is therefore an important part of using your account to its best advantage. Just what does your custodian do?

Your custodian is a neutral third party, much like a title company. The custodian will maintain your SD-IRA and facilitate any transactions in it. Self-directed IRA custodians maintain forms and agreements which the IRS and the U.S. Department of Labor regulate. Among the items they require and assemble and execute on the account holder's behalf are operating agreements, offer documents, promissory notes, certificates, and others which establish and prove investment ownership by the individual IRA. The custodian will help up ensure compliance through extensive documentation.

SD-IRA custodians set up accounts for their account holders. They facilitate transfers and rollovers from other IRAs, 401 (k)s and other retirement plans. They accept and document account contributions. Importantly, custodians are neutral third parties, who act on instructions from the account holder. Their function is administrative, and they must be a qualified third party per IRS requirements. They do not dispense financial, legal or investment advice.[xxvii]

As already mentioned, all income and expenses that relate to real estate investments in an SD-IRA must occur via the account. Custodians receive and record any investment income for IRA assets and disburse and record expenses for the assets. Even if the IRA account holder has check-writing privileges, the checks are directly tied into the SD-IRA account.

Custodians also execute account holders' instruction to buy or sell an asset, to facilitate transfers or distributions, and to dissolve the account if desired or necessary. In tandem with this, the custodian completes tax reporting for IRS Forms 1099-R and 5498. Custodians must comply with all federal and state regulations pertaining to custodial duties.

Account holders also receive IRA statements, often issued quarterly, which detail transactions, assets and cash in the account, and list income and expense details. Plus, each year your IRA must report a fair market value (FMV) of your IRA assets. Your custodian provides and houses this form, which is due on January 31st every year. Fair market value is the value assessed at the end of December (31st) of the year before the form goes out to you.

As you can see, the custodian plays an important role for SD-IRAs and the investments they contain. Many of these are administrative. Your custodian choice thus becomes the first important one as you build your team. For your convenience, this book contains a whole section to simplify your custodian choices. Please see the next section and the appendix for this.

Keep in mind that the SD-IRA custodial landscape continues to expand and morph, mainly because more custodian options than ever before are now available. And custodial costs are now favoring the consumer more. However, the changing landscape demands that you verify our cheat sheet. At press time, research that went into helping you evaluate custodians was up to date, but please know that information changes fast. I therefore do not guarantee the accuracy of the information. You must verify it.

Personally, I changed custodians three times. Customer service is a biggie for me. I like a live person who is knowledgeable and friendly to answer my questions when I call versus sitting in a phone tree, having to leave messages, or getting call backs days later. My trust in the custodian increases when they treat me as a valuable customer. The same applies to timely turn around of forms. It may be different for you. You decide.

Custodial forms

The IRA custodian you choose supplies you with forms that range from opening an account, to rolling over funds, to authorizing investments in the account, to expense payments, contributions and distributions. Such forms are accessible and downloadable on the custodian's website.

Alternatively, you may call the custodian's customer service line to find out and confirm which form is the correct form to use. The custodian then either directs you to the download section of the website or sends you the forms, usually via email. Once you are familiar with the forms and how to fill them out, using the custodian's website if easier and faster because you will be able to DocuSign documents most of the time.

SD-IRA custodian overview

Now that you already know so much more about self-directed IRAs, let's move to the next step. Which custodian should you consider for setting up and maintaining your account? This is an important question because there are now many custodians in play, and it is sometimes very difficult to figure out distinguishing features and services. Finding a custodian can be an exercise in due diligence all by itself.

Lest this become a distraction for you and cause you delay, I have put together a list that gives you differentiating features for several custodians. You will still have to do some additional work, but the included comparison saves you a great deal of time and effort.

Some custodians have been around for much longer than others. Some have specialty experience. Many allow for real estate investing and some deal in other alternative investments. Some have great customer service, others lack it. Various custodians offer investors checkbook control, usually via a SD-IRA-specific LLC, while others serve as the account's administrator and handle all transactions and payments.

The right custodian for you is a choice that depends on your needs and what you want to accomplish with what investments. It took me two prior custodians until I found the perfect one for me. That is why the comparison you see here is valuable as a starting point. It is imperative to follow up by reaching out to the custodians that appeal to you via email, website contact form, or phone. Combine them so you know which works best and what fits your preferences.

Important differentiators between custodians include ease of contact, custodian call back or response times, knowledgeable, website functionality, turnaround times, and fee schedules. Fees are important because they affect SD-IRA returns. SD-IRA custodians are specialty entities and fees are higher than at a brokerage at any rate. If your account balance is larger, fees may have less impact on your returns. Whether your balances are large or small, ensure that you understand the custodian's fee schedule and its impact on the account.

Finally, assess how trustworthy the custodian is. Online reviews can help you do this when added to conversations with and responses from the custodian. Sometimes, word of mouth recommendations also benefits you. You can get those by attending real estate investment groups or from other capable professionals in the field. Never rely on those alone and do your own checking.

Also look at how long the custodian has been in business and customer ratings. See additional evaluation criteria in the done-for-you comparison. Keep in mind that this space is constantly growing and our effort to give you the most up-to-date information still requires you to do your own homework about the custodian. A comparison of selected custodians is available as a bonus to you. This compilation is for informational purposes only and implies no endorsements or recommendations. Please download it at www.sdirarealestateinvesting.com.

Start by analyzing the companies via visiting their websites, calling them, and reading on-line reviews. Customer service, processing, fees, check-writing privileges, etc. differ with various custodians. If you are like most consumers and investigate custodian reviews on-line, brace yourself: many custodians appear to have poor on-line reviews and that fact hinders consumers.

Although more custodians now exist, it remains difficult to evaluate them. The best way to do so is to dig into their offerings, understand their process, and glean the way they communicate. This is not foolproof, but it is the best way to complete the due diligence process in finding a custodian. Compare service, response times, and the answers to your questions.

Lastly, the focus of this book is on real estate investing in your SD-IRA. For this specific purpose, it is important that the custodian has experience in real estate investments. They may have a department of staff dedicated to real estate investments. Ask them and find out whether they also handle commercial real estate investments and what those involve when dealing with this custodian.

You may also want to know whether their real estate team comprises Certified IRA Services Professionals (CIPS), which are retirement account professionals. Certifications show these professionals are adept at retirement account issues and requirements and are knowledgeable about real estate investments in the account as well.

Once you decide on a custodian, set up the account according to your investment objectives. This is important because the custodian must handle all financial transactions that relate to the investment asset—per IRS rules.

Financial transactions the custodian handles include buying or selling an asset in your self-directed IRA, paying asset expenses, and collecting rental income.

Okay, you decide which custodian is for you. Now, let's set up the SD-IRA account.

Setting up your SD-IRA account

Either call the custodian or go to their website to set up your account. Custodians require that you pay set-up fees and fund the account. You can either send your contribution or roll over funds from an already existing account. It may take up to ten business days to complete the account set-up. Ensure that your account has sufficient initial funds in it when the set-up is complete.

Some people set up their SD-IRA only to have it sit and languish without using the account. Don't be one of them. Use the account to the fullest extent you can, especially since you will pay fees to maintain it. Most custodians assess fees every quarter and they can add up. Therefore, fund the account with your full annual contribution and start investing in it. It is hard to overstate the power of funding your SD-IRA account with yearly contributions.

You will see how accounts can grow with consistent contributions. Please see more details about contributions under that heading.

Opening an SD-IRA

You may decide to roll over a 401 (k) that has a healthy balance to an SD-IRA. Please only do this if you are no longer with the employer where the account lives. Otherwise, you lose employer contributions.

When rolling over the 401(k)

your first decision regards whether to pay taxes on the rollover and establish a Roth IRA or to pay taxes later and establish a traditional IRA. This is true unless you have a Roth 401(k) to which you contributed with after-tax dollars and on which you owe no taxes. The account must be at least five years old to qualify.

For our example, we will assume a $100,000 401(k) balance, though your balance may be considerably more. 401(k) balances differ by age, by contribution amount, by salary earned, and by investment growth. [xxviii]

The assumption of a $100,000 regular 401(k) balance rolled over into a self-directed Roth IRA would mean you pay tax on those holding when the conversion occurs. Your tax bracket determines the tax rate that applies. Let's assume you fall into the 24% tax bracket and would therefore pay $24,000, bringing your Roth SD-IRA account balance to $76,000. Note that additional fees might apply to facilitate the roll over and to set up a new account. We will ignore those in this case.

Many shy away from paying these taxes, unless the upside to doing so is considerable. Often it can be, depending on the investment choices and their return on investment. Our examples apply to your new shiny Roth SD-IRA, in which your profits grow tax-free.

You identify a 3 bedroom/2 bath single-family home that costs $60,000 and do your homework on the property. The property is turnkey, in a good neighborhood and in a location that has job growth and low property taxes. Monthly rent is $1500.

Outright purchase	$60,000
Closing costs	$3,000 (3–5% of purchase price)
Monthly income	$1,500
Property management	$ 150 (on average 10% of monthly rent)
Property taxes	$ 50 (% of property tax rates vary by state.[1])
For this example, the assumption is 1% per month.	
Vacancy allowance	$ 75 (5% of monthly income)
Maintenance and insurance	$ 450 (30% of monthly income)
Cash–on–cash return	14%

Your profits grow tax-free in your Roth SD-IRA, while you incur tax liability on the profits in a traditional SD-IRA.

Should your SD-IRA hold fewer funds than necessary for an outright property purchase, you could option property or paper or invest in more conservative, more passive investments, such as notes and tax liens. The option money your SD-IRA puts up makes up a much smaller amount than for an outright purchase. More information and examples follow in the section that addresses these assets one by one. Finally, you can pursue a non-recourse loan. Please read more about non-recourse loans in Chapter 7.

SD-IRA Investing Steps

Next are the steps to invest in real estate in your SD-IRA.

1. Open your SD-IRA account. I recommend a Roth IRA versus the traditional IRA.
2. Identify the investment.
3. When writing the contract for the investment, your IRA custodian must be the buyer, not you.
4. Send a copy of the contract to your custodian.
5. Complete the custodian's investment form and request the earnest money deposit, made out to the seller. Ask the custodian to mail this check to you.
6. If you are using SD-IRA funds to close the transaction, fill out another investment request form. Ask the custodian when they need this to facilitate on-time closing. In this form, direct the custodian to wire the funds to the closing agent.

These steps apply to investing in a property in an account without check-writing privileges. Some steps are distinct if you have an account with check-writing privileges. Ask your custodian what they need from you and all the ways you can use your check-writing privileges.

Further, these investment steps apply to buying or optioning a property. I have already addressed *subject to* transactions and advised against them when starting out because they can trigger UBIT. The above steps do not apply to *subject to* transactions.

If you are selling a property in your SD-IRA, the closing agent must write a check or wire the money to your custodian. It should read like this: Custodian Name FBO, Your Name, Roth IRA, Account Number. This is important. The check or wire cannot be in your name.

Even if your custodian keeps records on your behalf and issues regular account statements, keep track of the transactions you do. Notate the asset (name), the transaction date, the transaction amount, and the Return on Investment (ROI) if applicable. Doing this will make your life easier.

What assets work?

All IRS-approved investments work in self-directed IRAs. Our focus in this book is on real estate, one of the IRS-approved asset classes. Investments in your SD-IRA are distinct from contributions. They are not synonymous.

Contributions are the allowed amounts that account holders may deposit into their Account. They are subject to annual caps. Please see the section about contributions for details. Investments, on the other hand, are assets account holders purchase with SD-IRA funds with the aim of growing that investment by creating profits. The two are distinct.

You may already envision the many profitable real estate deals you can make in an SD-IRA account, but before you count them, start at the beginning. Once you complete the first transaction, move on to the second one and so on.

One word of warning about making countless such investment transactions in your account: doing over 3-5 investment transactions in a short period may trigger an unfavorable IRS response. If the IRS decides you are running an investment business, the IRS may tax such transactions as business related transactions. Tax rates for that IRS determination run quite high, sometimes up to 50%.

Obviously, this result is undesirable. To avoid this, stay away from making over 3-5 real estate transactions in your account. Stay within the lower numbers of that spectrum, even because how the IRS assesses whether your transactions fall into the *business-related* category is unclear. That means doing so rests on the IRS' interpretation.

The good news is that you and your spouse and other family members who have an SD-IRA can invest in real estate in their accounts as well. When you and your spouse have separate IRAs, it might be a good idea to partner on the deals the accounts hold. That way you can equally share in the expenses and the profits and evenly grow the accounts. Doing this is one secret to a happy marriage. Set this up by instructing your SD-IRA custodian to implement a 50/50 arrangement.[xxix]

A final comment in this chapter is about managing your real estate investments in your SD-IRA account. Your function regarding real estate investments extends to mostly administrative tasks and overseeing the investments. Refrain from physically managing the properties to avoid self-dealing.

This encompasses doing repairs or renovations yourself or property management, etc. You can hire contractors and other professionals to do work, approve such work, and pay for services rendered via your SD-IRA. In the same vein, you must pay any income from the property or expenses that relate to it through your SD-IRA. Your tenants pay rental income to the SD-IRA, not to you personally.

Chapter 6: Real estate investment strategies in your SD-IRA

Ω

Buy on the fringe and wait. Buy land near a growing city!
Buy real estate when other people want to sell. Hold what you buy!
- John Jacob Astor

Making our money work harder than we do ultimately defines investing. All investors pursue growth and leverage of what they have. Benjamin Graham's classic *The Intelligent Investor* about value investing outlines the idea that investing is a business and therefore treating it as a business. He combines this fundamental idea with using market fluctuations to one's advantage and with buying an asset when it is worth more than its price in the market. His famous student, the fabled investor Warren Buffett, claims that *a hundred years from now [these ideas] will still be the cornerstones of investing*.

You may have picked up that both Graham and Buffett referred to stock market investing in particular, yet these fundamentals equally apply to all investing
, including in real estate. Most famous real estate investors, like Sam Zell and Donald Bren, made their considerable fortunes in commercial real estate.

While commercial real estate often produces huge portfolio increases that accompany many higher risk investments, most of us have little interest in risking our retirement monies unless we have expertise in this asset class.

The good news, however, is that real estate is one of the best investments in modern history. This includes other real estate asset classes that we're taking a closer look at here.

1. Buy property outright with cash in your SD-IRA.

While doing this is fine, this strategy only works if your account has sufficient funds in it to do so. If the account has little money in it, employ strategies that require almost no money but will turn profits. Let's go to these now.

1. Buying property with a loan (debt) in your SD-IRA.

Yes, you can buy property inside your SD-IRA with a loan. However, these are specialty loans, which are non-recourse. [xxx] Only a few lenders will offer them. Consult the *Resources* section for some lenders in this niche.

Non-recourse loans have special requirements, including higher down-payment amounts. Although you create leverage in your SD-IRA when utilizing a non-recourse loan, such debt may also trigger Unrelated Business Income Tax (UBIT). Consult your custodian or CPA about possible IRS treatment and implications.

1. Wholesale properties

When wholesaling properties, you become the middleman and make a profit by putting a property under contract, then assigning it to another buyer. That means you will never truly own the property. However, to put it under contract you must put up a good faith deposit, which may be as low as $100.

Next, you find the actual buyer who pays you an assignment fee. That fee becomes the profit you net in your account.

1. Lease option property. Cashing out.

In some ways, this is like wholesaling. When lease optioning a property, did you find that property and put it under an option contract with the ability to assign the contract to another? The lease option agreement provides you the option to either assign the property to a buyer or to buy it yourself. For investors who have limited funds in their self-directed IRA, this is a great option to make a profit from real estate.

With assigning it to another buyer, you control the property without purchasing it yourself. The option agreement usually requires a good faith deposit of $100 or more, also known as consideration. That stands in stark contrast to with how much the property would cost if you were to buy it.

In this scenario, the lease option investor profits from an assignment fee, which flows into the self-directed IRA. Doing a lease option agreement also considerably mitigates the investors' risk because only $100 is actually at risk. Those $100 must count directly from the self-directed IRA account, meaning your custodian issues it to the seller's title company. While you can pay the money directly to the seller, using a title company is superior.

Consult the appendix for many lease option contracts.

1. Optioning paper.

The same process as in number 4, the one you just read about. In this case the option is for paper, such as a mortgage note or deed of trust.

1. Buying paper and reselling it

Instead of optioning paper, you can buy it outright, then either hold it or resell it. Buying paper can be very profitable. By buying and reselling it, you may purchase a note or first or second mortgage, then resell it to another investor at a profit. Or you can also option the paper and do the same here. Clearly, this takes know-how. For starters, it helps to understand mortgages, the mortgage industry and how money moves. This strategy also requires having a buyers' list. The strategy is hands-on and active.

1. Passive paper investing.

Here you become the bank and leave the legwork to active note investors. Passive note investing might be a great way to enter the field, but return on investment ranges between 8 to 12%, depending on the note. That is unlikely to make you rich but allows you to deploy your money into passive (for you) assets while making reasonable returns and deciding on other investment options with higher returns.

1. Tax lien investing

Another option is to become the bank and collect interest on your money. You help counties stay afloat by fronting money their property tax payers fail to pay. Counties pay a wide range of interest rates. Their bidding systems aim to pay as little interest to investors as possible and rules apply. However, informed investors are still generating sizeable returns. More details follow in the next chapter.

1. Partnering on property investments.

Partnering on property investments is a great option to grow your portfolio. You and your spouse ought to have individual SD-IRAs on which you can partner. Make it a 50/50 split and instruct your custodian accordingly.

Or you may partner with other investors. Here the split is what you and the other party agree to, depending on what each party contributes to the deal. Perhaps you are seeking an investment partner with cash to fund a deal, while you contribute in other ways. Make sure you have a written agreement in place and instruct your custodian accordingly.

You can also partner with yourself. What I mean by this is investing funds sitting in the SD-IRA alongside funds you have outside of it. Determine the split and instruct your custodian about it.

Note that no matter what kind of partnership you employ, the percentage of the split (ownership) must match the expense percentage.

Now that you know all these details, remember that your SD-IRA can hold assets short-term, long-term or both. It bears repeating that your own home or a rental or commercial property you already own cannot become part of the IRA. The IRS considers self-dealing. That's a no-no.

All these real estate strategies and the assets that complement work, though they depend on how much money is dispensable in your account. They also depend on your personal risk profile, on exit strategies, and on market environments.

Cash Flow and Appreciation

It's never too early to plan for your future. Real estate investments in an SD-IRA can help build your retirement nest either through cash flow or appreciation profits, or through a combination of both. Appreciation is often a bet on market direction and that direction must continue up to benefit from it. Cash flow, however, is a more immediate way to profit.

Run all your numbers to ensure the investment generates enough cash flow to net a profit. The numbers are part of completing the due diligence for the asset. Read the section about doing your homework in Chapter 7 and work through the checklist to screen the asset. Then use the ROI calculator to ensure that your cash-on-cash return is a minimum of 15%. This applies whether you pay all cash for the property, or you finance it. Your cash-on-cash return will be lower if you buy all-cash assets. But strive for the highest cash-on-cash return to cover all costs and still make a profit.

A property's cash-on-cash return helps you make money when buying a property versus just betting on appreciation. Many buyers who bet on appreciation during the boom before the Great Recession lost their shirts. Appreciation is great when it happens, unfortunate when it doesn't, and foolhardy to rely on. This applies to all investment property types. Remember, make money when you buy. If you are waiting for profits when you sell, your wait may be arduous and long.

Someone who wants to quickly grow their account might look to fix and flip properties. The fix-and-flip strategy is one of buying low and selling high. In this scenario, the investor buys a fixer property in a neighborhood with high market values that continue to climb. Colloquially speaking, the neighborhood is desirable and because of this the fixed-up property generates profits. Profits often are substantial and range from $25,000 on up but remember that profits correlate to higher risk.

The fix and flip strategy require property and market knowledge and the ability to complete the necessary repairs through qualified professionals. Now, if you are a contractor or someone who is handy with house improvement projects, the strategy instantly may appeal to you. This excitement subsides when you realize that you cannot do repairs yourself and pay yourself for them for any property in an SD-IRA. Doing so falls under self-dealing. This means the professionals you hire must renovate the property. Your SD-IRA account must have a sufficient financial cushion to do so.

Once the property has been repaired, the next step is to find a buyer. In an up market, this should not be a problem, so long as you bought the right property, complete the right repairs, and correctly price the property. In a down market, the sale of the property might look quite different. Also take into account how much time, money and expertise fix-and-flips require, components that are often bigger than investors believe they are.

Plan for all these contingencies. Dig deeper into fix-and-flips by reading a few books about what they involve. You could also spend thousands of dollars on coaches and programs. Most of them will relieve you of your money without providing more than some of the outstanding books and blog posts available for a much smaller investment.

Much to think about with fix-and-flips, right?

You might be more comfortable with a buy-and-hold property, a strategy that relies on steady income. Buying and holding is more conducive to growing your account balance over time, instead of making a sizeable chunk of money as quickly as possible. In the buy and hold scenario, you can hold the property until the market is conducive to a profitable sale, thereby profiting from income and appreciation alike. Your risk in this strategy is lower than in the fixing and flipping.

I told you to plan for shifting markets when employing the fix and flip strategy. Let's add another piece to this: you could use the buy and hold strategy after you fix the property. Evaluate whether that would work as a viable back-up strategy for you, should flipping prove difficult. Run all the numbers to assess this.

You may also find that certain asset classes work better than others. Single-family homes remain in demand. They represent the largest real estate asset class in the United States.

Single-family homes

Single-family homes make up over 60% of real estate stock in the United States. They are plentiful. People live in single-family homes they own, but over 35% percent of single-family homes are rentals. That number is likely to remain constant and even increase, though most Americans desire to own a home.

The premise of single-family home investing is to rent out the property. Demand for single-family home rentals is high and such homes are easy to locate. Because of this demand and those seeking a home as their residence, construction activity for this asset class remains high as well. A single-family home in an SD-IRA cannot be the account holder's residence and must be an investment. The investment must make financial sense, something so these investors' single-family home holdings fall into the affordable range. While luxury homes are a potential niche, the numbers for them usually make little sense for investment.

U.S. corporations and investors selling to investors have figured this out and bought up single-family home inventory across the country. This trend started at least a decade ago. Corporations, including Warren Buffett's Berkshire Hathaway HomeServices arm, hold huge single-family home portfolios. Some of these homes are affordable, while others are luxury rentals.

All this to tell you that single-family homes, while easy opportunities compared to other real estate investment assets, are a way more competitive investment class than they used to be. What that means is that great deals are now much harder to find in this category. Corporate owners and other investors have driven up the prices of this inventory.

The numbers vetted through exquisite research are more necessary than ever. Please take that to heart. I mention it because for any investor who lives in a high-property and high-rent value city, like New York, Seattle or San Francisco, a value that is, say, a tenth of the values customary here seems a fantastic bargain right off the bat. Unfortunately, this often turns out to be false.

Long-distance investing seems easy. The internet lifts all investment boats, except that finding pertinent and true information is more labor-intensive than surfing the net. That is why many beginning investors buy marked-up properties from other investors. They rely on these other investors as the experts. Maybe they are, but even then, there is no substitute for true market knowledge. Such knowledge and expertise come from seeing and inspecting the property, its neighborhood and city and so on. Consult the due diligence chapter and cheat sheet to dig deeper.

How then do investors find the perfect single-family home?

For one, gather as much knowledge as possible about the market that appeals. I recommend doing so independently from the homes' evaluation sheets that other investors or sellers provide. The internet is a great starting point but go as deep as you can. Take a trip to the location where the potential investment is. Do so by yourself or with your family, not with the now popular caravan tours. These tours aim to sell you on pre-selected homes. Yes, those tours are fun, but they hardly make the participants investors. To re-iterate, know the market in all its aspects backwards and forwards through your own analysis.

Next, understand the property. It might need repairs. If so, what are they? What is the price tag for them? Thoroughly inspect and find the right professionals to assist you. Understanding the property also means knowing the property in relation to its neighborhood. Does it fit in with the other homes? Is the neighborhood developing and if so, how?

Pay attention to any construction you see, then find out what the city is planning for the neighborhood. This could include infrastructure upgrades, new parks and malls, and grocery stores. For example, seeing a Whole Foods[xxxi] market popping up in a neighborhood indicates neighborhood gentrification.

Existing and changing demographics are equally important. They show the job landscape and how it relates to home and rental affordability in the market you consider. These metrics tell big stories: whether locals can continue to live in that city or neighborhood or whether they are now priced out of it. Whether outsiders are moving into the location and why. Whether the location is a tech hub or up and coming as one, or whether it is a retirement haven.

All these distinctions make a difference, sometimes a huge one. Assess them to the best of your ability. Parenthetically, many locations that appear in articles on the *best place to live, best places to retire, best places to invest* lists show old news. These places appear on such lists after others have done what they promise.

In tandem, it is important to know the ratio of renters to owners in the location you are considering investing in. From there you glean the pools of renters and/or home buyers in that market. This, in turn, helps understand trends and the competition. Vacancy rates and planning for them become more intelligible and finding a competent property manager is easier. Last but not least, this information puts potential rental ranges and what tenants get and expect for such rents in perspective.

While there is more to consider when entering the single-family home investment market, this is a fabulous start. Assess your risk upfront. That way, you can mitigate it in intelligent ways, something that is always important. Remember that the SD-IRA must pay all expenses and that all income from the investment assets must flow into the account. For your retirement real estate portfolio, it is essential. Gambling in an SD-IRA is a poor idea.

Once the right single-family home investment appears and enters your SD-IRA portfolio, seek the next one and build from there. Entertain owning properties in one or two different markets for better diversification. After taking a long-term consistent approach, single-family home investing becomes a profitable asset class in your SD-IRA portfolio.

Condos and Tenancies - In-Common

Condos and Tenancies-In-Common (TICs)[xxxii] can be excellent investments because these units are part of a building with other individually owned units in it. The building's property management company not only maintains the common areas but often also manages rentals in the building. In effect, property maintenance is much easier for both condos and TICs. Of course, the owner of a condo or TIC foots the unit's maintenance bills and pays Home Owners Association (HOA) dues that include common area maintenance. Additional fees apply to property management services, if available.

Condos and TICs have Covenants, Conditions and Restrictions (CC&Rs) that rule the properties. Many of them contain clauses about what types of rentals they allow. The CC&Rs usually exclude short-term rentals, usually rentals for less than six months. They want to keep the buildings stable and shun Airbnb and other short-term rentals they view as *hotel* use. Other clauses apply, so read all applicable HOA documents before purchasing.

If condos and TICs appeal to you, crunching the numbers is important to ensure cash flow. Condo investments make the most sense in prestigious buildings in sought after locations. In San Francisco, such condos are often modern bells and whistle high-rises in SoMa or high-rise buildings in historical neighborhoods along the waterfront. In many other communities, sought-after locations include properties by lakes and golf courses.

TICs often are in buildings with up to ten units in many neighborhoods. While TICs are rentable, most are owner-occupied and often necessitate considerable owner involvement in the building's management.

Condos and TICs are more complex to evaluate because of building rules, added costs, and rental restrictions. They can, however, be good investments even then, so long as they create income for the investor. Crunch all the numbers, including the unit's price, rental income, property tax, insurance, HOA dues, management fees and others. Use the formula in the ROI calculator to ensure the property cash flows. Find out all you can about the neighborhood, the property market, the rental market, including demand for the rental you would offer.

Multifamily

Multi-family properties comprise 2-, 3-, and 4-unit buildings. When buying such a property for your SD-IRA, you mitigate various risks because you hold more than one rental unit. Just to re-iterate, this is an investment property, and you cannot house-hack the property. Let's look at a multi-family example that aligns with the ROI calculator.

You buy a duplex, say, in Indianapolis, Indiana. See the example breakdown on the following page.

Price:	$150,000
Down-payment	$60,000 (40% of purchase price)
Closing costs	$4500
Loan	$90,000 (30 years at 4%)
Mortgage/month	$404
Rental income:	$1750 per unit = $3500 total
	$42,000 per year
Taxes and insurance	$1545 (1.01% taxes) + $1000 per year = $2545
Vacancy and maintenance	$12,600 (30% of income)
Property management	$2400 per year (10%)
Total expense per month	$1463
Monthly cash flow	$2037

When buying a multi-family property with a non-recourse loan, as in the example above, the goal is to create equity, cash flow, appreciation and depreciation. In our example that works well. Investments grow over time. Note that UDFI applies to a property financed with debt (a loan). Re-read Chapter 2 for relevant information about UDFI.

As previously mentioned, leverage works in the investor's favor here. Investors also benefit from reducing expenses and increasing profits through scale.

Commercial Real Estate

Commercial real estate is a vast field. It comprises everything from office buildings, to retail buildings, to specialty categories such as apartments, hotels, nursing facilities, mobile homes, funeral homes, parking lots, storage units and the list goes on. Each of these is a category unto itself.

Investments in commercial property require more experience and expertise. From a pure price tag perspective, commercial property costs more money and loans that most times are property specific. The list of items to investigate is longer, more involved and costlier than for residential property.

The upsides to investing in commercial properties include high returns and profits, lower operating costs scale, and possibly residual income. That is because these properties are much bigger than a single-family home or a condo.

Commercial properties require more money and time to vet. Sometimes loans and even finding such properties can be challenging. It therefore pays to connect with other successful commercial real estate investors, lenders, and Realtors®. Building a viable network to find and execute deals is vital.

Equally valuable is arranging the financing in advance. That includes finding lenders with the right loans and understanding which properties they finance. Some investors find out the hard way that a lender that sounds so good to them only finances certain commercial real estate property classes versus the one the investor seeks.

What matters most to commercial property lenders is cash flow and location. Lenders also factor in economic development. These factors often make it easier to qualify for a commercial loan, depending on the investment asset. Still, most investors partner with other investors on such properties.

Any commercial deal may take something like six months to put together because there are so many layers to consider. Some of these include zoning, environmental evaluations, upgrades and renovations, tenant profiles, surrounding infrastructure and development, and legal considerations.

Commercial real estate investments might make sense for anyone with expertise in one of the commercial sub-categories I mentioned or for someone who has a sizeable chunk of money to deploy. You could also partner on a commercial deal with someone who either has the expertise or the money. In that case, you must make complimentary contributions to the table and work out a mutually agreeable and beneficial partnership agreement.

Remember that many partnerships

are unequal and carefully considered how a partnership would and could work. Know what you are getting into and with whom.

On the flip side, commercial real estate investments carry higher risks. Besides the higher cost, book cost to carry such a property is also higher. Capital outlays are much higher than for other, more run-of-the-mill investments. However, it is possible, especially through a partnership, to invest in commercial real estate with less money. Each investment is different and requires its own evaluation.

Other considerations that affect commercial real estate are that properties carry economic risk. COVID-19 comes to mind with many office and retail buildings sitting vacant. Even in regular times, a commercial property that is vacant may take a long time to find the right tenant. And of course, all of this affects the actual value of the property, meaning that selling the property depends on these factors to net a profit.

The best way to approach commercial real estate investing is by doing one's homework and mitigating risk through analysis of the markets, the trends, the potentials, and any applicable government regulations. The numbers can be amazingly persuasive and certainly make investors wealthy.

In addition to partnering with those with fewer funds available in their self-directed IRAs, crowdfunding platforms or via syndications offer other possibilities to acquire commercial properties or an interest in them. In either case, investors pool their money with other investors for a certain property which the sponsor vetted. The same thing applies to syndication. Crowdfunding platforms often allow investors to come in with very little money, though some of these platforms are open to accredited investors only. Syndications, on the other hand, are mostly open to accredited investors.

Investing in a commercial real estate deal via a crowdfunding platform or a syndication by definition makes the investment passive. The sponsor, of course, gets paid a management fee and various other fees throughout the life of the investment. Read all the fine print about the investment, the way the platform or the sponsor makes money, the way the investor makes money, the project timeline, and the project details before committing funds to it.

If you wish to read more about commercial categories and subcategories, please read my book title, finding profitable deals and other books about commercial real estate. For our purposes here, we will go into the apartment subcategory because it is most similar to multi-unit building investing.

Apartments

Apartment buildings belong in the commercial real estate investment category. Although they are residential buildings, their scale makes them all about income and the ability to cut expenses more easily. Compared to a single-family home or two, a multi-unit building with say four units, apartments sometimes comprise twenty, hundred and more units. Buildings that have between 13 and 99 units our midsize apartment buildings. Those over 100 units are large size apartment buildings. The sheer number of units requires running the apartment building as a business. The more units a building has, the greater the potential to lower associated costs.

Yet, compared to other commercial real estate investments, apartments can both be easier to manage and require less expertise than, say, hotels or specialty facilities. The bigger the apartment building, the more important good property management becomes. Choosing an excellent property management company is essential. By the same token, per unit costs, whether property management, vacancy, or maintenance costs, are often lower. Scale lowers expenses and multiplies returns.

For investors who have insufficient cash for apartments in their SD-IRAs and for those who are uninterested in pursuing a non-recourse loan, other investment options follow. These include controlling a lease, holding or selling an option. Leases in this context mainly apply to commercial property. Real estate options can work for both residential and commercial properties. Let's turn our attention to them now.

Real Estate Leases

Real estate leases are a great way for the investor to profit with little money on the line. They make the most sense in commercial real estate. Leases are complex and powerful legal instruments, which allow investors to control a property without owning it. The best fit for leases is an investor who has experience in leases and who possesses the ability to be an efficient and effective landlord. In an SD-IRA, the investor cannot do this to him- or herself but can partner with a party outside the account to achieve the goal.

Investors can find office or retail space landlords who hold properties they would rather not deal with. During the pandemic, many commercial landlords sat and continue to sit on vacant buildings. Office and retail vacancies increased by ten to fifteen percent from 2019 through 2021. Those vacancy rates continue to climb.

Some commercial landlords either have no interest in finding a solution themselves, have deep financial cushions, or have little interest in being landlords. Clearly, investors who understand leases must find a landlord who is interested in a solution to vacancies. That means they must have a checklist to find out what properties work for their purposes. Their outreach to landlords must stay on track with that.

They must locate landlords from whom they lease the property with the right to sub-lease it to tenants. This can be a win-win negotiation for the landlord and the investor, so long as the lease is airtight. Doing this requires little capital from investors, but there is upfront work in assessing the property and its uses, finding landlords open to a master lease solution, and lining up the right tenants for the property.

Investors who become master tenants run a business. They are landlords, not agents of the property owners. For that reason alone, property owners might find this solution for a property sitting vacant appealing. The arrangement reduces owner liability for the property and allows for income streams for both the property owner and the master tenant (the investor). Conversely, investors benefit from lower risk as well because they do not own the property. Property repairs usually remain the responsibility of the owner, not the master tenant.

The lease should be a long-term lease in this arrangement. It may also contain a clause that allows the master tenant to purchase the property down the line. Such leases generate passive income into an SD-IRA, if correctly set up. However, as always, evaluate how a master lease could work for you by engaging a competent CPA and attorney. Plowing ahead without professionals who understand the implications of an SD-IRA is foolhardy.

Options

Options are another way for real estate investors with little cash to make money in their SD-IRA accounts. Investors who either buy options or sell them may purchase a specific property or sell that right to someone else. The right to do so creates only that. It does not obligate the party to execute the options agreement. If the investor passes on the option to purchase the property, he forfeits the option money. Nothing more.

Property options sometimes start at only $100, though they may run into the thousands depending on the property. An option applies during a specified time period, something that gives the party time to do their homework on the property, to figure out the financial details, and to implement an exit strategy. The buyer and the seller usually set the option at a predetermined price for the property, which may be below market value when property acquisition occurs. The party who purchases the option controls the property at a small fraction of the cost of ownership. This allows for the party to either purchase the property themselves or to assign the contract to another party, which then executes the sale.

Many investors make money with the assignment strategy as they charge other investor buyers a fee. The fee often is in the $10,000 to $15,000 range, though can vary to lower or higher amounts. Sometimes, the option premium or fee correlates to the properties after repair value (ARV) value.

This kind of arrangement can make a lot of sense for wholesalers. They source the properties, then sell them to a rehabber on an option agreement. This rewards them for finding the properties and putting them under contract with the owners, something that takes both persistence and negotiation skills. Ideally, this scenario would also benefit the rehabber because it saves him time and money otherwise spent sourcing the properties. If structured correctly, there is still plenty of financial upside for the rehabber. What we just discussed can apply to residential and commercial properties.

For example, a potential buyer pays the seller an option of $20,000 for a property worth a million dollars for which the buyer negotiates a price of

$750,000. The option has a specific term which we set at three months for this scenario. The buyer either exercises the option or it expires once the term is complete. During those three months, the buyer might investigate whether zoning allows for a new development of the property, whether he can get the loan needed to buy the property or lines up another buyer to whom he sells the property on option.

He sells the option at a higher premium to the other party, making a profit. If he cannot find another buyer, to get the right financing, or if he learns that his development plans for the property are not workable, he lets the option expire and the seller keeps the option premium. Other variations on the theme exist.

You can probably see that options have wonderful potential and that investors ought to have a system in place for them. This is especially important because many optionees end up walking away from the property instead of buying it. Market knowledge, developing a network of potential buyers, and screening these buyers are preliminary steps to succeed with the option strategies. Because optioning a property may mean that the first potential buyer ends up not buying the property, the temptation to take advantage of people who from the outset are unlikely to execute the option exists. That may seem like an income generating strategy without end, but it is unethical and can get you into hot legal waters to boot. Please don't do it. Your reputation is too precious to take this chance.

Next are lease options that apply to commercial real estate. More sophisticated instruments, these usually apply to becoming a master tenant, as discussed earlier in this section. The master tenant, through the option agreement with the property owner, controls the property. He uses the property as per that agreement and puts sub-lessees into the property. His agreement with the property owner ought to be transparent, meaning that the owner knows how the master tenant will use the property. No fudging here unless you wish to invite trouble.

Now you might wonder why a property owner, or a landlord would agree to an option versus just selling the property on the open market. While many reasons exist, the main one often is that the property will not net enough to meet owner obligations in the current market environment. Vacant property creates problems for the owner. Those problems range from vandalism, to carrying costs, to no income.

For these reasons, lease options can be powerful income producing avenues. Investigate them further, then use them in your investing arsenal if you believe they are right for you. Always remember that doing this in your SD-IRA can substantially increase your bottom line as long as you properly manage them in the account.

Land

Most people think of real estate as the building or the structure, also known as the improvement. The land underneath is, in fact, real estate. Land is a finite asset which has intrinsic value. Anyone who lives in a high value, high cost real estate market can attest to this, although it is often not spelled out.

In San Francisco, where I work and live, many buyers are hamstrung when considering how much more they can get for their money elsewhere. Most lack the understanding that the land on which the home they want to buy sits is the true asset. Yes, the home has value, but one can replace or rebuild homes, while the land is irreplaceable.

Many investors specialize in land investing, a niche that contains sub-niches. Some sub-niches are land development, re-zoning, land leases, sub-dividing, and more. Land can be very profitable, but you must have a plan for it. As a real estate investor newbie, I bought land as a long-term hold asset. While that seemed like a good idea, the approach entirely relied on future appreciation, which unfortunately never happened. In the meantime, annual taxes and SD-IRA asset fees continued, amounting to big negative numbers. Consider that you will pay taxes and fees on any land you hold and that you need the staying power to hold the asset long enough to make a profit.

Assess whether opportunities exist to generate cash flow from the land you consider owning. The parcel might be perfect for a solar lease or for billboard leases or for farming. You could even seller finance the land to create cash flow. Investigate what any of these income-producing avenues involve. That way, you will be a happier land investor than I was.

Note Investing

Note investing comes in two flavors. One is active note investing; the other is passive note investing. The focus here is on passive note investing because it is an easy way to generate profits in your SD-IRA. First, though, a word about the differences between the two.

Active note investing is a business in which the investor finds and negotiates notes. These can be performing or non-performing paper, either first or second mortgages. Active note investing requires knowledge, experience, and professional networks and relationships. All these components make it time-intensive, and the learning curve is steep. Mortgage and finance professionals might opt for active note investing but are unlikely to run that business in their SD-IRA.

Passive note investing is more suitable as SD-IRA investments because the investor simply becomes the bank for an active note investor. The money loaned generates interest that flows into the investor's account. The interest ranges between 8% and 12%, though variations exist.

Real estate secures these notes. Underlying real estate guarantees the money loaned but read the fine print of any agreement you sign. The note itself is either a mortgage or a deed of trust. Both are promissory notes, official financial instruments and agreements. They are written debt instruments which obligate the indebted party (borrower) to pay the lending party under certain terms, all fixed in the note. The most important function of these notes is to secure the lender against default by the borrower.

Loan terms also differ. Some of them tie your money up for 6 months only, while others extend to 2 or even 5 years. The notes I hold are either for one or two-year terms. That is because a 6 month term means seeking the next investment almost immediately and the associated fees add up to boot. Five years, on the other hand, ties up the investment funds for too long for my taste. However, either shorter or longer terms benefit investors, depending on their situation.

For example, an investor who wants to take advantage of a different investment opportunity in another eight months may decide for his money to work with a shorter-term note. An investor who holds various other investments and plenty of cash in the SD-IRA may be happy with the 5-year term of a note.

Note investing opportunities range from smaller investments of $10,000 to $20,000 to larger investments of $100,000 or more. Some are open to unaccredited investors, other only to accredited investors. The Resources section provides additional details to get you started.

As always, vet the party with whom you do business. Investigate whether a mortgage or a deed of trust backs the note. If there is a default, differences exist about the specifics to foreclose

for a mortgage versus a deed of trust. Although a passive note investor would not foreclose, it is important to know this. Generally, foreclosing on a mortgage requires court approval while doing so on a deed of trust does not. In addition, ensure that no other liens exist on the note. A title company and/or real estate attorney can do this work for investors. Some custodians will require this at any rate. Whether custodians require a title company or an attorney to facilitate the transaction in your SD-IRA, always use one anyway.

Passive note investing can be a splendid start in real estate investing in your SD-IRA, especially for more conservative investors. They also serve well when the investor has yet to identify other opportunities or to an investor who is just beginning.

Tax Liens

Tax liens sound appealing, and they can be. You can invest in them for as little as $100, but a more realistic amount resulting in acceptable returns is $5000 or more. Tax liens are ways to help local governments stay afloat. They fill government coffers with needed funds. Local governments lack these funds, which are their due, because a property owner is delinquent in paying property taxes. For investors, tax lien investing represents the opportunity to make a rate of return on the amount extended to governments.

Many people believe that the opportunity tax liens offer is that they might get the underlying property for little money. Few investors will experience that blessing. Most will not. That is because most property owners eventually pay their taxes. Only a small percentage of properties end up in the portfolios of investors who paid the properties' taxes. Still, it's a nice perk when it happens.

Tax liens offer a wonderful opportunity to generate passive income and help local governments stay afloat. Many counties now offer tax-defaulted property lists online and most have a bidding system that investors must follow. The system can be complicated, so educate yourself about the states and counties you are interested in acquiring a tax lien for. Every county has a unique process, often different terms and pays different interest rates.

The ability to generate a return that ranges between 8% and 50% is a boon to investors.[xxxiii] The municipalities set the interest rates they will pay and they either have a bidding system or a highest offer system in place. Other terms, including timelines and expiration of the liens, apply.

If the lien is not redeemed, the investor must either clear the property's title or foreclose on it. This process, once complete, means that the investor then owns the property. Foreclosing or clearing title of the property to which the lien attaches requires up to $5000, so investors do well to have this sum available in their account.

The next important thing to know about tax liens is that they are much more popular than even ten years ago. Now, corporations with large bidding power have entered the field. That means they often bid out smaller investors but don't give up. Instead, find out where they would be profitable for you and how to proceed there. You could do this by reading a book or by taking a course on tax liens that gives you all the details.

Even then, tax liens involve considerable legwork. The investor must vet the property to which the lien attaches. It also helps to understand the market the property is in and whether other liabilities exist for that property. Experts in the tax lien niche therefore offer training, membership and coaching. The *Resources* section contains a few ways to start with tax liens.

A quick search online will show you which states are tax lien states and which ones are tax deed states. Although tax deed states also offer opportunities to investors, bidding on tax deeds requires sizeable cash sums. To get started, our focus is on tax liens for this reason.

Your curiosity might pique by now. That is great because tax liens can provide a wonderful boost to your portfolio. And once you have a portfolio of several such liens, you might find that tax liens are the way to go.

Start with tax lien investing by

1. Choosing a state and county or counties to invest in.
2. Call or email the county or the municipality of interest.
   a. Some counties' websites also work for this.
   b. Connect to county websites via https://www.naco.org/.
3. Sign up for their tax lien list.
   a. Many counties charge a fee for tax lien lists.
4. Find out when tax lien sales happen there.
5. Educate yourself about the bidding process.
6. Register for the sale.
7. Research the properties.
   a. Put the due diligence list to use.
   b. Understand what you are bidding on.
8. Pay any deposits and auction fees required.
9. Bid on chosen liens.
   a. Know the property's value and your bottom line.
   b. Avert emotional bidding.
10. Wait to collect your interest and any applicable penalty amounts.
    a. If you are the winning bidder.

11. Adhere to time frames.

    a. Track your tax lien investments.

12. If the lien is not redeemed, foreclose on the property.

    a. Your SD-IRA must cover the foreclosure costs.

13. Reinvest.

14. Continue to build your tax lien portfolio.

Any of the real estate investment strategies you just read about might work well for you in your self-directed IRA. You might eventually mix and match strategies, or even come up with some of your own. In either case, any of these investment strategies and property types can work well in your SD IRA portfolio. You decide which one or which ones are the right ones for you. I encourage you to start with one particular property or investment type and learn all about it before adding other investment types to your portfolio.

Syndication and Crowdfunding

Syndication and crowdfunding represent other investment opportunities in real estate. Both pool investor money to accomplish more. Both are also passive investments that tie up the investor's money for a minimum of one year and usually longer.

Investing in syndications or via crowdfunding platforms facilitates benefiting from participation in large commercial projects. These are projects for which the investor may otherwise have insufficient funds. Risk may also lessen in syndication real estate investing because the investor pool shares it with the fund's management.

There are differences between syndications and crowdfunding platforms. Syndications have professional management in place, while this may or may not be true for crowdfunding outfits. Most syndications and an increasing number of crowdfunding platforms accept accredited investors only. Given that 10.6% of all investors are accredited in the United States, ordinary non-accredited investors must look elsewhere.[xxxiv]

Some crowdfunding platforms, however, allow investors to come in with as little as $100. Those investors do not need to be accredited. However, that low investment threshold affects returns as management and administrative fees might eat them up. It is imperative therefore to figure out at what amount an investor stands to make a profit. That may be at $1000 or $10,000 or $100,000. It differs from platform to platform.

All this brings us back to doing our homework, in this instance checking out the syndication and crowdfunding platform. Assess how long they have been around and what their track record is. Read the fine print about how your money goes to work and who receives payment first. Learn all you can about the project and run your own numbers. What risk mitigation strategies are in place and how could you further lower your risk for the investment? Also understand the process that either the syndication or crowdfunding platform has in place. And of course, they must allow for SD-IRA investing and should be familiar with that process.

Once you do your homework and still like the project and what it offers, these investment options can generate nice returns in your SD-IRA.

Chapter 7: Locating the Right Investment Properties

Ω

When you want to do your homework, fill out your tax return, or see all the choices for a trip you want to take, you need a full-size screen.
—Bill Gates

Choose and buy the right properties.

Here is a quick overview of the process for buying, managing and selling an investment in an SD-IRA.

Another one that shows what the process looks like with an SD-IRA LLC in place.

In the next schematic, your LLC sits with your custodian and the custodian completes IRS-reporting.

Your
SD-IRA
LLC

Buying
property
or paper

Selling
property
or Papper

You, the
LLC
manager

Optioning

Expenses

Income

Finding the right property investments for your SD-IRA is like panning for gold. Lists of hot markets proliferate the internet and other investment sites. By all means, check them out, but know that places on these lists usually have been bid up already. If you are okay with the left-over scraps in these locations, that's fine, but you probably want to do better. At least I hope so.

Another point about these lists is that you can expect other investors arrived there first—before you. That means they bought properties there in the earlier stages and drove up prices by selling these homes to people who can afford to pay them. Such folks might be out-of-towners who are moving to the city or town, or other investors who often want to make guaranteed rental incomes. Most of the time, the locals in such places are being priced out and either move on or even become renters in these investment properties.

I believe that this investing style is socially unconscious and opt for communities that have somewhat slower housing price growth, while still showing job growth and other favorable factors. This is one small way to mitigate the huge affordable housing crisis that continues to sweep America. I will profit a little less and do my part. You may disagree with me and that is fine.

Affordable housing and real estate investing intimately link together. Today, home ownership is out of reach for many Americans. Per the National Association of Realtors' statistics for 2021, 74% of white Americans own their homes, while only 49% of Hispanics and 45% of African Americans own their homes. These percentages suggest long-standing disparities between American ethnicities and social classes. They pervade almost all sectors: jobs, education, opportunity, fair treatment, crime, housing, and the list goes on.

They also fail to show the bigger picture of many changes wrought in America. One such component is that housing affordability now affects all social classes. Today's homeowners' children may never own a home, unless they rake in huge salaries and their parents provide down payments or leave their homes to them.

Affordable housing is a catchword of our times, yet the issues have been with us since the 1970s, and we need solutions fast. Investors can make a difference and provide solutions that extend past sheer profits. Some have done so and perhaps you will too.

No matter where you stand on affordable housing, always contemplate how your investment decisions affect your community, the community the investment is in, and the fabric of our society. Ask yourself whether your real estate investments positively contribute. Are they both profitable and sustainable?

Choosing and buying the right properties involves where to find such properties. Ready-made easy investing is at your fingertips either with the *best places to buy lists* just discussed or by finding other investors who are selling you their products. Both come at premium prices, even if the price points appear low to you. If you follow my lead, more homework is necessary. Few, if any lists, exist for such locations and you will have to ferret them out by other means.

Live where you want to live and know that if you want to live in certain locations, others probably want to live there as well. What are the places you want to live in? What are the places and locations you hear others speak about? What locations do you read about in articles and magazines? Which of these places are still up and coming versus already being gentrified?

Ask yourself these questions to see whether any of these places and locations are beneficial places for real estate investment. I bring this up here because you've probably heard about the creative class, those folks who move to where they want to live because they have the freedom to do so and are less tied to specific locations for their jobs. Read Richard Florida's 2003 book titled *The Rise of the Creative Class* to learn more.

The implications of the aforementioned are that real estate investing can happen where you want to live and where there is still room for growth. These particular growth patterns, indicated by movements of the creative class, also influence property appreciation in those locations. The same applies to communities that attract retirees and second home parties.

Naturally, people living in high cost-of-living areas with high real estate values are attracted to out of state or out of area properties. Entire businesses have sprung up just around those types of properties, which are often sold as turnkey investments. Be aware, however, that often these properties have a huge markup from what you would find other properties selling for in the same market or even the same neighborhood. It is a buyer beware scenario and requires a lot of investigation and savvy. In my experience, such properties require much more homework than if the property were in your own backyard.

Wonderful out-of-area or out-of-state real estate investment opportunities exist, but they are far fewer than advertised. If you buy an advertised turnkey property, another investor likely is making a profit that way.

Often turnkey means the investor has improved or rehabbed that property and now sells it for a higher price to another investor or an out-of-towner. That price is often higher than what the locals would pay for the property, simply because it may not be affordable to them.

Or someone could appeal to you on the basis of low risk and offer guaranteed rents. Read the fine print on those guarantees, then vet every single number through your own rental rate analysis for the property, its neighborhood and so on.

I recommend visiting the location and checking out the neighborhoods and prices. However, do so on your own versus going on one of those investor tours, unless you like hype and feeding frenzies.

On that note, many other investors, real estate agents, sellers and even builders cater to out-of-town and out-of-area buyers, counting on the unfortunate fact that most buyers are uninformed or poorly informed. Buyers in those categories are easy prey. The only way around this is to research the market slated for investment in versus relying on others to do so. Know the market, the laws, rules and regulations in that market, comparable properties, neighborhoods and so forth. Never rely on those who want to sell property to you, at least not without having done your homework.

Californians are especially vulnerable because they come from a state where property values are sky high. In comparison, values in other states seem like absolute bargains. Whether that is true depends on all the factors discussed in this book. Homework becomes indispensable and by homework, I mean one's own. The internet contributes to easy property picking scenarios because now bargains appear right on the screen. No travel required.

Except, are these properties bargains? Maybe, maybe not. Yes, the internet makes our lives easy and complicated at the same time. Make sure you understand what you're getting into and what you're getting. Compare prices locally versus to the prices of the location where you live.

Promotions that pronounce that they take away risks an investor may experience when investing out-of-state usually carry fine print. One such promotion said the offeror guaranteed rents for a year, mitigating possible vacancies. However, you may pay a premium, usually factored into a much higher property purchase price than the area and neighborhood commands. Or they calculate returns a certain way. You must understand and vet both the property pricing and any return calculations. Vet the offeror and their financial stability and strength. Will they be able to support these wonderful promises?

Finally, real estate investing appeals to the imagination. It holds sex appeal. I mention this because the sheer image of being a real estate investor is pervasive. Seminars, courses, subscription programs and mentorship programs draw followers and attendees for this reason alone. Offerors of all such programs either have property to sell to investors or even offer easy financing, another potential pitfall for investors. Easy financing is so seductive that some investors, often new to the game, purchase a property that offers it even when the property otherwise makes no financial sense.

The upshot of the foregoing is to help you become aware and circumvent at least some of these problem areas. Please read the chapter about due diligence, also known as doing one's homework, to set you up for success. Due diligence is an important topic and we will address what to do and how to do it right after a brief detour about funding your property portfolio with loans inside your SD-IRA.

Taking out loans in a self-directed IRA.

Taking out loans to fund your properties in your SD-IRA is a possibility that helps grow your holdings. Many SD-IRA account holders buy properties with their own funds versus with loans. This will make more sense after you read about the loans permissible in self-directed IRAs.

The SD-IRA accounts permit only non-recourse loans, loans with which many ordinary consumers are unfamiliar. Non-recourse loans differ from recourse loans in that the borrower is not personally liable for the loan. No personal guarantee is in place. Your name does not appear on the loan. The loan is in the name of your SD-IRA.

The collateral and the income of the property secures the non-recourse loan. Here, the real estate you purchase with the loan in your SD-IRA is the collateral. For example, in case of default or foreclosure, non-recourse lender can only go after the asset to which the loan applies. The lender cannot go after the IRA account holder or the other assets in the SD-IRAs account. Recourse loans are loans for which the borrower is personally liable. These are the loans customary for property you buy outside your self-directed IRA.

For lenders, non-recourse loans are riskier loans than their more common cousins. For this reason, they are specialty loans that charge higher interest rates and require bigger down payments. Only certain lenders offer non-recourse loans.

Non-recourse loan products depend on the type of property. For example, they vary according to whether the property is a single-family home, a commercial property, or a multi-unit property. Most non-recourse loans have restrictions on the type of property you can buy with them. These vary from lender to lender as well.

However, the commonality shared by all non-recourse lenders is that their loans are available for investment properties only. Of course, the IRS prohibits personal use of the property, anyway.

To date, few lenders offer non-recourse loans, so line one or two up before you need them. Get a head start by investigating the following lenders: They offer non-recourse loans and are knowledgeable about self-directed IRA investing.

Explore non-recourse loan options by finding a knowledgeable and savvy non-recourse loan mortgage consultant. Your mortgage professional ought to be well versed in SD-IRA real estate assets and what each requires. Set everything up with the mortgage professional ahead of time. Remember, the account is paperwork intensive, and things can move slower than you'd like. A competent non-recourse loan mortgage consultant can save you time and headaches and make certain you qualify for the loan.[3]

A non-recourse loan makes the most sense when your IRA is small or when it holds insufficient funds to invest in real estate. Find out what non-recourse loan products a lender offers. Get all the facts about what requirements, restrictions, terms, fees, and timelines the lender has. Research and compare with non-recourse lenders. Start with the *Resources* section, as you are unlikely to find a non-recourse lender by calling your bank.

Also, remember that taking out a loan incurs additional charges and fees that your SD-IRA must cover. Inspection and appraisal fees, as well as closing costs. If you ever borrowed money from a lender, you will be familiar with various other fees.

Be aware that when borrowing a non-recourse loan in your account, unrelated debt-financing income (UDFI) applies. I discussed UDFI in the section about the cons for SD-IRAs. From that, you may recall that UDFI relates to any property you finance through a debt instrument. A certain amount of the income for the loan-financed property is taxable.

Erring on the side of caution, let's re-iterate verbatim:

If you purchase a $100,000 property with $50,000 of your SDIRA funds and $50,000 in debt. This fifty-fifty split means that the portion you financed with debt represents the portion of your net income to which UDFI applies. You annually pay taxes on 50% of your net income on this asset.

However, UDFI[xxxv] is more complex than stated in this simple example. Some exceptions and exclusions might apply to your situation. You may also have to file a Form 990-T with the IRS, something your custodian would request from you at tax time. Consult with your tax professional to understand the UDFI specific to your situation.

Real estate investment know-how

Real estate is one of those subjects in which many people consider themselves experts. Almost anybody has opinions about real estate, often strong ones. Unfortunately, opinions and expertise often stand far apart. What papers, magazines, internet blogs and so forth publish about real estate contains limited information. Sites like Zillow, Trulia and Realtor.com make their money by connecting consumers to real estate professionals who pay a pretty penny to appear on these sites. In doing so, they cannot be and are not real estate experts. Even Zestimates, Zillow's proprietary property valuation tool, eventually drives consumers to agents and mortgage professionals. That is because the tool is unreliable and often way off the mark. This is so by design. The service these sites provide is that they are good starting points for consumers.

The Multiple Listing Service (MLS), whether residential or commercial, is a proprietary network only accessible to licensed realtors®, usually in the state and area where they work. Most of the listing information that appears on the consumer-facing sites just discussed syndicates from the MLS. Over the years the MLS has existed, and individuals and companies have attempted to *disrupt* the industry. The latest are Proptech and Fintech companies who operate through technological innovations, though they can only do so by feeding on the system they claim to disrupt. That means these companies are brokers and agents just like all others in the industry.

You get the idea: to get pertinent and timely information, it is necessary to find outstanding agents who know their markets like the back of their hand. Even if you have access to websites, usually membership sites, which provide you with some good information, real estate is a team sport. It counts to know the markets and there are many of them. For example, people sometimes ask me *How's the market?* and my response often is *Which one?* San Francisco proper has many neighborhoods and sub-markets plus many property types. Other markets are the same.

Location, market research, property type, property valuation, local rules and regulations, and financials are only a few topics a professional can help with. The most important component there might be that the person you engage with is honest and forthright. Smart real estate investments depend on professionals who aren't just out to sell you something and instead look out for your interests. That is the true meaning of any fiduciary.

Now you may say that no one can look out for you the same way you can. Maybe so, but you still rely on other professionals, including your SD-IRA custodian. You can, of course, become a licensed professional in one or more of the areas that require expertise yourself. Many real estate investors eventually become realtors® for all the reasons mentioned in the first several paragraphs and to make more money.

In case you are happy with your profession and want to remain a real estate investor, read as much as you can about the field of real estate. Follow this with more reading about the property classes that interest you. Take webinars, attend seminars and educational events about them. Connect with professionals and with people already doing what you want to do. Alternatively, start with a lower-hanging fruit investment such as a single-family home or a passive note backed by real estate. You will learn about the ins and outs of the investment and about all the items you read about in this book.

You may even become an expert. I am afraid there are no shortcuts to becoming one. In either case, your best option is to do two things: 1. To locate and engage the right professionals and 2. To do your homework on every real estate investment in excellence. Deal analysis, aka homework, is next.

Deal analysis

Take calculated risks. That is quite different from being rash.—General George Patton

Profitable real estate investing relies on doing one's homework. Combine that with effort, time, knowledge and understanding of the market. Yet, for some reason, many Americans today believe that they can cash in on real estate with none of these in place. Take my advice and banish the thought of real estate gold on the streets. Little to nothing happens without work and profiting from real estate is no exception.

Do yourself a big favor when following the *do-your-homework* invitation. The reason for this is that you won't be gullible, or at least to a lesser degree, and your chances of falling prey to real estate schemes and scams become almost nil. Plus, you will be able to build a sustainable, profitable portfolio. No shooting in the dark. No speculation, unless you consciously choose speculation. Fewer or no nasty surprises. You're in control.

Although your custodian executes and facilitates all investments in the self-directed IRA, you still need to do the due diligence on the asset. All real estate investing requires analysis of the asset, its financial numbers and return potential and how to negotiate and navigate the transaction. This entire section deals with conducting due diligence well.

There is a world of difference between residential real estate and commercial real estate property analysis. The latter takes more time and money to put together an in-depth analysis. Think of due diligence as both the ability to make intelligent investment decisions and as an important avenue to mitigate any inherent risk in the investment. In fact, think of doing the homework on any property as a big part of your risk/benefit analysis.

However, even though all that is true, please remember that all investments carry risk and depending on the specific real estate investment that risk may be high or low.

Well done and thorough due diligence mitigates risk because it covers many properties and transaction risk factors. This leads to prudent steps that reduce or eliminate such risks. Sometimes it means walking away from the property and the transaction.

If you want to take out a loan, in-depth analysis is the key to securing it. Just make sure you understand the lender's specific requirements and what types of properties the lender will loan on, something we discussed in the previous section.

Assess all property and property-related details up front. What that means is for you to complete your homework about the lender, the property, the baseline for the transaction, the financials, the timeline, and other applicable parts, such as necessary repairs and renovations. Whether you invest in property that is close to home or in property that is in other states or even in other countries, complete your analysis to the largest level you can. Some items to know right off include:

- Applicable real estate laws and practices in the location (city, state, country) in which you invest.
- Understand the tax rates and calculate them into your returns.
- Select a support team such as a realtor, a lender, an inspector, a contractor, a title officer, an attorney, and a CPA.
- Vet your team.
- Investigate the market dynamics where you are investing.

- Plan an overall strategy.
- Develop an exit strategy.
- Look at good deals only.
    - What I mean is that your investment baseline and the return the investment have to match. The numbers must make sense.

Once you've done this, find possible properties and start evaluating them. You may find these properties on your own, through a realtor, through another party, or any other way that works for you.

Let's say that your realtor provides you with listings in the market you choose and within the parameters you set. Go through those listings and run your own numbers for them. Clearly, the listings will provide you with certain information, such as the list price and maybe the rent the property commands, and possibly whether the property needs repairs. Once you know the market, the property neighborhood details, and any pertinent trends for that market, you will know at least some of the potential the property has as an investment for you.

Although your realtor will help you assess the market and its movement and provide you with other important information, I recommend you run your own numbers as your first step. One reason for this approach is maintaining a great relationship with your realtors, which precludes inundating them with evaluation requests. Another is that you will understand the property in the market much better when you do so. And yet another is that your realtor may not be a real estate investor himself. Although a realtor® who is also an investor helps, it is unnecessary. You will still benefit from the services.

Once you identify which listing is a potential investment for you, communicate with your realtor and ask him or her to run numbers for you as well. I recommend you do both steps in the order I just delineated and do so without telling your realtor that you've already run numbers. Compare both sets of numbers once you have them.

To make the number analysis for the property easier for you, please see the property investing sheet in the Resources chapter. The rental property return on investment (ROI) formula you see below is excellent for assessing residential properties. Assessing commercial property is a complex and time-intensive process. I recommend your commercial real estate broker guide you through what is necessary for the commercial asset class.

Claim an additional expanded due diligence list as a complementary download at www.sdirarealestateinvesting.com[1].

Here is the formula the due diligence list plugs in, and how to calculate your own numbers. You also ought to budget for a property inspection report, which runs several hundred dollars, depending on the property.

Purchase Price

Closing Costs

Rehab Costs (if applicable)

After Repair Value of the Property (if applicable).

Rental Income

Vacancy Rate (in%)

Repairs and Maintenance (% of rent)

Property Management Fee (% of rent)

Annual Property Taxes   Varies by county.

Consult *Resources* section.

Use the ROI calculator which is a bonus for you. Just plug in your numbers and it does the calculations for you. Go to www.sdirarealestateinvesting.com[2] to download it.

If you opt for a non-recourse loan in your SD-IRA, also calculate:

Loan Amount

Interest Rate%

Loan Terms in months

Monthly Mortgage

Payment (P&I)

Use the return-on-investment worksheets or calculators when you receive listings. Run your numbers that way first. Clearly, you need to research some additional data, such as the rental range in the neighborhood the listed property is in and what the tax rate is for its location.

Once you have identified which listing could work for you, the next steps are to verify where the property is located, to investigate its neighborhood, to understand its site characteristics, including its zoning and any other land use features, as well as whether the property complies with its legal use description or possesses non-conforming features. You want to know whether a property is up to code or whether you eventually must bring it up to code.

Verify the property's lot size and shape, floor plan, square footage, number of rooms, bedrooms and baths, garage, fencing, decks and patios, etc. If the property has views or other location-specific features, verify those as well. Note any deferred maintenance apparent to the eye.

Follow this with a professional inspection once you determine that the property is worth pursuing. While you could do an inspection before making an offer, this takes time and costs money. Write the offer first and include an inspection contingency in it.

Establish the property's rental value and rental demand for it. For single-family homes and condos, the rental values should amount to no less than 1% of the property asking price. If the property needs repairs, add those to the purchase price and then calculate 1% of that total to see what the rent should be.

An example of this would be if you were to purchase a property for $200,000 and have repairs of another $25,000, the total would be $225,000. One percent of this amount comes to $2250. The 1% rule which comes in handy when reviewing rental property, especially when taking on debt for the property. The aim of this rule is to ensure that the rent will cover the mortgage payment on the property. This may or may not apply to you when investing in a self-directed IRA. However, I believe that the 1% rule is still quite valuable when purchasing the property all cash because it provides a baseline for the investor.

The 1% rule is great as a general guide, but it must be combined with figuring out your rate of return on the cash you are bringing to the table. The reason for this is that you could have very high costs such as maintenance fees and HOA fees, which could eat the property's entire rental income. To mitigate such an effect, your return on investment for cash on cash should be anywhere between 12 and 15%.

Here's what that looks like. If you were to put down 30% of the $225,000, which we assumed for the previous example, your cash in the deal would amount to $67,500. To calculate the return on investment for this amount, take the annual income the property will generate and divide it by the total cash invested. For our example, let's assume that the property meets the 1% rolled and generates an annual income of $27,000. Divide the $27,000 by the $67,500 and your cash-on-cash investment percentage will be 40%.

This return sounds amazing, and that is because it does not yet factor in taxes, annual operating expenses, annual debt service costs, or vacancies. For a more realistic cash-on-cash return, you must therefore subtract these expenses. Now your cash on cash returned looks quite different, doesn't it?

This number is therefore helpful only in fairly straightforward investments versus, for instance, multifamily unit investments or commercial investments. Even then, it provides a limited picture. For example, depending on how much equity you have in the property, cash on cash return rarely accounts for that. It also does not factor in property appreciation.

Still, it gives you another metric to evaluate property with and assess whether your investment strategy will work. It is a quick way to weed out properties that are of no interest to you and for which to complete a deeper analysis. That makes it a wonderful tool to use when you're doing a lot of different property analyses on a consistent basis.

For multi-unit investors, the income ought to exceed 1% at any rate. If it doesn't, take a step back and reevaluate the property from various vantage points. When evaluating multi-unit buildings, review the building's income for the past two or three years, any vacancies during that time, the rent rolls, the expenses, and so on. For a multi-unit building, also calculate the gross operating income and deduct its expenses to get the net operating income. Once you have that, find the gross rent multiplier (GRM)

by dividing the sales price by the total annual rents. Then compare that gross rent multiplier with similar properties in its neighborhood.

You can also calculate this gross rent multiplier with potential rents the market will bear. Just make sure you know the rents in the market the property is in support of. Rents vary by location and amenities. - Gross rent multipliers show whether a property is overvalued and that might be something to consider.

CAP rates are also important when evaluating commercial property. CAP rates indicate future rental income and can range considerably. Simply put, the lower a cap rate is, the greater its future income expectation. I draw your attention to cap rates here because they can become important indicators of value and investment opportunities. I could write an entire chapter about cap rates in their application, but for our purposes this suffices. The most important component of a cap rate is that it helps you assess the level at which your investment property generates positive cash flow.

A quick word about appraisals is that appraisals provide limited information. They depend on one of three approaches to assess a property's value: the comparable sales approach, the income approach, and the cost approach. Those are valuable but they do not factor in whether the property has a marketable title, the property's parcel map, existing easements and encroachments, or whether all property systems, such as plumbing heating and cooling, and electrical systems, are sound. Therefore, never rely on an appraisal by itself. Hire competent contractors to assess property systems. You could also hire a building inspector to do this.

All of this to tell you must know other things besides a property's market value. These include assessing whether the property will generate sufficient cash flow, whether you may expect the property to appreciate, or whether you can add value to the property, and if so, where and how.

This goes along with the next part of the due diligence process, which involves reviewing disclosure documents. Laws that require disclosing what sellers know about their property are now on the books in many states in the U.S. Sellers and their agents must disclose known property defects and more, but disclosure laws vary by state. [xxxvi] In addition, some sellers, such as banks when they sell foreclosed property or courts selling probates, are exempt from many disclosures. The reason for this is that they rarely know the property. Once again, inspections will be your best friend in these scenarios.

Once you identify a potential property, allow your agent to do the background work on the disclosure side. You should still read the disclosures and prepare questions to ask your agent and the other party, but your agent is likely to know much more about what to lookout for. Keep in mind that seller disclosures help you understand the assigned value of the property but that disclosures can be faulty. Items may be missing. Some properties may also not require the same amount of disclosures, if any at all, as others do.

Inspections alongside the disclosures are your best friend when considering a property. Accompany your inspector to the property. It will amaze you how much you'll learn about the property, the neighborhood, common issues, the market, etc. You should always view the property yourself and conduct a complete walkthrough with your own checklist in hand. Doing so is prudent.

The worksheet above includes items that may not apply to you in your self-directed IRA, but having a comprehensive worksheet helps down the line. If you evaluate non-recourse loan, you can then apply this worksheet. Just remember that the tax consequences that will offset alone in your account need to be in addition to this worksheet.

I already mentioned the importance of inspections. If you decide to take a loan out for a specific property, all lenders will require both an appraisal and an inspection. Those are just good risk management. Do an inspection, even if you buy a property outright. While it will cost money to do an inspection, it may save you many headaches down the line and help you understand what you are getting into and what the property needs. Inspections facilitate better decisions.

Inspections may reveal potential issues and drawbacks a home or property might have. They also show ways to upgrade the property. They provide guidance on property value, improvements, renovations and how financing and financials for the property work. Think of inspection as insurance.

Inspecting property allows you to analyze the property in more depth before committing to purchasing. For this reason, many contracts have inspection contingencies in them, but even if you buy a property *as-is*, do an inspection. The cost of several hundred dollars, the exact amount of which depends on property type and size, is well worth it. Inspections can be excellent tools for negotiations. They can also indicate that walking away from the property is the best option. Professional property inspections are necessary for investors, even if they are contractors themselves.

Much to do, do you agree?

Once you do this and develop a system for doing the homework, your real estate investing will take off. You will get practice because it often takes evaluating many properties before you find the right one. You will learn about the business from an investor's perspective. You will also get ideas, some obvious, some not so obvious, how to improve the property. For example, you could improve the property by converting usable space to more living space. Or you can add pizzazz by adding landscaping, natural light (if possible), adding appliances or storage, and many more. One underrated immediate improvement is often a deep cleaning of the property.

If you'd rather skip these steps, if you could invest via a crowdfunding platform or via a source that offers turnkey properties, mostly single-family homes. In both instances, the party selling the property or raising funds for it completed the due diligence. However, you still need to verify their findings and investigate the offeror. See the appendix for some *done-for-you* options.

Finally, clients often ask me how much time the due diligence requires. The answer is that it varies. The first step of running the numbers with the ROI calculator is fast and easy and shows the investor whether to complete additional due diligence. There is no need to continue doing homework if the numbers mis-align. Use the tool as a weeder to identify for which properties you will need to complete due diligence.

Do as much of this work upfront as properties move fast in the marketplace, especially the great ones. Work with your team. If you decide to submit an offer, do so with contingencies. The due diligence process has many facets and often continues throughout the transaction. Waiting to complete it before writing an offer may therefore mean that none ever solidifies. And no investing happens without writing offers.

Do the best you can, then make your investment decision and make a move.

Adding value

People who add value to others do so intentionally.
I say that because to add value, leaders must give of themselves, and that
rarely recurs by accident. - John C Maxwell

Adding value is about understanding the market the property is in and what people who are either buying your property or are renting this property type are seeking. Here is a case in point: if you are a flipper, you need to know the neighborhood your property is in, and whether the property profile, that is the number of bedrooms and baths, the appeal, the renovations, fit what buyers, in this case presumably homeowners, want. Once you know this, you could, of course, do exactly what your competition is doing and just paint the property and cosmetically upgrade it. While that is fine, it also means that you will blend into the competitive landscape versus standing out from it.

How then can you achieve that, meaning standing out from the competition?

To do so, start by checking out your competition and the buyers they want to attract. Obviously, that also means knowing how they are approaching renovating their properties. Getting to know your competition is an enormous step. Not only will you see what works and what doesn't, but you will also get ideas of how to improve upon your approach and how best to attract buyers.

For example, notice how the property's landscaping fits in with the neighborhood. Does it hold an appeal? Could it benefit from improvements that are easy and low-cost? Does your competition offer anything special besides the home and its amenities? If so, what are they offering? Perhaps a way to qualify the buyers in a fast and efficient manner or a home warranty when purchasing from them or allowing the buyer to choose certain appliances up to a certain dollar amount. There are many variations on the theme. You get the idea.

When renting a property, you similarly might stand out after surveying the competition and potential renters, then aligning this information with both the market and your own offerings.

The practice of surveying your competition, potential buyers and tenants, and understanding the market gives you a competitive edge. Among the things you'll learn are:

- The language which advertises the property.
- The locations of these properties.
- Amenities offered.
- Financing and terms offered.
- Property pricing and rental rates.
- How easy it is to reach your competitors via phone, email, etc.
  - Can you reach out to a live person?
  - Are they friendly, knowledgeable, and even persuasive?
  - How long it takes to get a response if you cannot reach a live person.
  - Are they marketing to you from thereon?
- Ease of viewing the property.
- How many renters and buyers are in the market for the properties you survey?

This list deals with initial research only, most likely via the internet, phone and email. I recommend taking the next step to complete the research. The step is to view the property inside and out, either by setting up an appointment or by attending open houses. This is a little more challenging during Covid-19, but still possible. Take mental and written notes about the property specifics: floor plans, room sizes, views, lighting, upgrades, landscaping, parking, security, storage, and other features. Input the information on a spreadsheet for easy reference.

One of the important things you will learn is whether the property you own or want to own requires much or little maintenance. The same goes for tenants to whom you rent the property. When both the property and the tenants in it are low maintenance, management becomes easier, and your property usually becomes more profitable. You read about adding value to increase profitability elsewhere in this book. Completing what I outlined here defines the path to profitability.

I realize this is work, but it is worth it, if only because few sellers and landlords do it. When you do it, patterns will emerge, and you will see how to improve your offerings. While guessing can work, it has many flaws. The homework I suggest leads you to better decisions and strategies than you could ever arrive at through guessing and sensing.

Managing properties inside your SD-IRA

You just stay the course and do what it is that you do and grow while you're doing it. Eventually it will either come full circle, or at least you'll go to bed at night happy. - Jon Bon Jovi

The properties your SD-IRA holds require management. Managing the property may mean screening tenants, collecting security deposits and rents, issuing rent increases, and navigating vacancies and evictions. Remember that the property's income, expenses, insurance, and all other monies associated with the SD-IRA property must flow through the self-directed IRA. This is also true when you establish an SD-IRA LLC.

In effect, the requirement to manage the property in the SD-IRA account streamlines the process. For the most part, it makes managing the property easier. Everything is trackable or it should be. It also contributes to abiding by IRS rules. However, the appropriate management of such a property requires some planning or at least a financial cushion in the account.

Also remember that you cannot maintain and repair your SD-IRA properties, even if you possess the skills. This applies to everything from plumbing repairs, to mowing the lawn, to a new roof. Although you can opt to perform some property management tasks yourself, like screening tenants and formalizing leases, you cannot pay yourself for these services. Doing so can have self-dealing and engender consequences.

Unless you have only one property in your SD-IRA and live-in close proximity to that property, hiring a property management company and contractors is a better approach. Per IRS rules, they must not fall under disqualified party stipulations.

I know rules are ornery but these are fairly straightforward. While you ought to know the rules, keep your focus on growing your SD-IRA real estate portfolio so that you fall into the current 5% of Americans able to retire in comfort and style. Commit to growing the percentage of this group by doing your part.

Chapter 8: Tying It All Together

Ω

Trust your own instinct.
Your mistakes might as well be your own, instead of someone else's.
-Billy Wilder

Other considerations

All investments, including real estate investments, contain risk. Risk is a fact of life and almost everything we do. Risk and decision making intimately link. Decisions may turn out to be right or wrong, often years after taking the plunge. The same is true for non-decisions, which in fact are inadvertent decisions. When large sums of money are in play, many people either are proactive, make no decision for fear of making the wrong one, or put their heads in the sand just looking away. The latter two describe fear.

Though fear is human and understandable it, just like hope, is not a strategy for success.

The best way to address risk and fear is to face it or rather the possibilities it brings. Do all you can to understand your own motivation and approach, to uncover blind spots, and to learn. If these suggestions seem unrelated to investing, they are not. Once you honestly take inventory, move on to real estate investments that fit your understanding and style. Learn all about those and do your homework—always.

That is what I call intelligent risk taking. As you may be able to tell, this excludes speculation, including in real estate. Gambling proclivities are dangerous and cloud judgment. Read the next section about real estate scams to learn more.

Our discussion on risk is short and to the point. Consult any attorney or CPA and you will learn more than you ever thought possible about risk. Tomes have been written about the topic. The point of the foregoing paragraphs is to heighten your awareness, so your path is clearer and becomes passable.

Finally, the discussion about specific real estate investments would be incomplete without noting that every single estate investment category you read about here commands volumes of information. Consider the information presented here as an appetizer. Any real estate investment category that appeals to you demands more reading and education. Everything in real estate is continuing education.

You may learn more about specific niches by reading my previous books, or by reading books and taking courses from authorities who specialize in a niche of interest. I also offer presentations about real estate investing via

YouTube and a course on the subject is under development. Go to www.sdirarealestateinvesting.com[1] to sign up to receive notifications for new materials, books, podcasts, and webinars.

You may see that passive income is what you really like or find out that you would like more involvement in investment decisions. In either case, it is helpful for you to know as much about the property types and the homework involved in understanding the investment as you can. Once you've done that, start investing right away. Now let's move onto how to find the right investment properties for you.

---

1.   http://www.sdirarealestateinvesting.com

Avoid Mistakes and Scams

It's morally wrong to allow a sucker to keep his money. – W. C. Fields

It is painful to fall for a scam. It happened to me when I first started investing in real estate over a decade ago. You read about it earlier in the book: I paid a pretty penny for the lesson and licked my wounds until it became clear that uncovering the scheme would have taken many levels of deep investigation. Many scammers are quite sophisticated. They are well-versed in what their victims want and many who fall for their offerings are unsuspecting.

As a case in point, during the San Jose, California trial of the scammers against whom I testified, several of the parties there were were their neighbors and even friends! Of course, such trials rarely happen, at least when compared to the proliferation of schemes out there.

From a *lessons learned* perspective, the silver lining of this disagreeable experience is that you can learn from it and hopefully avoid finding yourself in the same circumstance. As I mulled over the experience, the realization that signs that something was off existed from the outset hit.

Recognizing the signs helps you stir clear of scoundrels and thieves; of those who are only too happy to collect your hard-earned dollars with smokescreen activities. Even if you discover it all and sue them or put them behind bars, it is unlikely that you will ever collect on any court judgment. Your assets seem to evaporate in the hands of these folks, who often live extravagant lives.

Scammers go after low-hanging fruit, especially when sizeable amounts of money are their potential reward. Easy and plentiful money for them is what they target. They have a *get-rich-quick* mentality, even if not betraying it to you. If you yourself share that mentality or are a speculator, you are easy prey. Real estate assets fit the description of tidy sums of money.

According to the Financial Industry Regulatory Authority (FINRA), many fraudsters target individuals who are optimistic, make their own decisions, possess above-average income and financial knowledge, are well educated, are open to new ideas, and have recently experienced financial hardship or health problems.

Take no chances. Learn the signs and do your homework on each real estate investment you acquire. The previous chapter is worth gold in this regard. Use it. Become a true investor. This alone creates a shield around you, one more difficult to penetrate by the uncouth.

Prudence applies in life and in investing. Today's scams and scoundrels are often quite sophisticated. They are bilking people who want to rake in cash and make a killing, naturally all without risk. A long list of Ponzi schemes targeting retirement savings attests to this.[xxxvii] Several charge excessive additional fees. By the way, many of these folks hold professional licenses which provide them legitimacy. Buyers beware.

Though it is close to impossible to control scammers, you can take steps to vet professionals and real estate investments, and to monitor your SD-IRA. Have a plan for your investments. Understand the risks inherent in the investment of your choice. Know your account activity and balance. Never succumb to pressure to invest. Always ask yourself whether the following fraud indicators are in play and walk away if they are:

- High returns.
- Low or no risk.
- Consistent returns.
  - Markets fluctuate, so consistent returns are unlikely and unusual.
- Income guarantees.
- Paperwork snafus.
- Not getting paid.
- Inability to get out of the investment.
- Investments that are not registered with the SEC or other regulators.[xxxviii]
- Unlicensed sellers. States usually require investment sellers to hold an appropriate license.
- Ostentatious seller behavior.

- Aggressive sales tactics.
- Focus on attracting other investors versus the investment.

Investors, of course, can report investments that appear to be scams to the SEC.[xxxix] However, investors only do so after their money evaporates and are unlikely to see it back. It is therefore better to understand the signs of potential scams and to do your homework upfront.

Scary stuff, isn't it?

Well, here are the other adages that serve real estate investors well aside from the foregoing list. Investors can steer clear of common mistakes by

- Never investing more than you can afford to lose.
- Continued learning about yourself as a person and an investor.
- Understanding the investments, you are interested in.
- Expanding your knowledge base of your investments.
- Valuing data and completing thorough homework.
- Establishing your exit strategy.
- Diversifying your investments.
- Understanding that all investments carry risk.
- Watching out for acting when you experience fear of loss.
  - Greed has taken out many an investor.
  - Establish criteria for when to get in, when to get out, what ROI you want, and protect your profits.
  - Pay prices that allow for upside, no matter your exit strategy.
  - Know that there are always deals around and believe the right transaction for you shows up at the right time.
- Understanding your risk tolerance—it goes hand in hand with many other commandments on this list.
- Mitigating investment risk.
- Understanding what financial security looks like for you.
- Understanding what financial freedom looks like for you.
- Matching investments accordingly.
- Building a cash reserve in your account.
  - The custodian will have a minimum in place because they would like to assure receiving compensation. However, you

may well need money to renovate or rehab a property or to facilitate closing costs, etc.

- ○ Figuring out how to leverage the resources.
- ○ Time
- ○ Money
- ○ Brain power
- ○ Your team.
    - One of the most important components of successful investing.
- Studying other's failures and successes.

If you, like me, are running behind on your investments to assure a great retirement, one with plenty of income and money to live a fulfilling, financially stress-free life, get started today and scale your investments. With investments of almost any kind, time is the factor that influences returns. That is, unless you know that SD-IRAs can supercharge your portfolio even when time is short(er).

Parting Thoughts

Ω

Your economic security does not lie in your job; it lies in your own power
to produce - to think, to learn, to create, to adapt.
That's true financial independence. It's not having a wealth; it's having the
power to produce wealth.
- Steven Covey

The Take-Aways

- Start with the right attitude.
- Keep your eyes on your goal.
- Stay within legal bounds.
- Follow IRS rules.
- Evaluate custodians—use the criteria in this book.
- Formulate a real estate investing plan.
- Open an SD-IRA and fund it.
- Use the account.
- Contribute the maximum allowable annual amount.
- Regularly review your account.
- Love to learn.
- Learn all you can about real estate investments that interest you.
- Do your homework.
- Build your investment team.
- Focus on the positive.

TV series mythologize real estate investing. It seems easy. Follow the lessons and the steps to stand apart from those who believe what they see and hear on TV. Sorry, there is little showing off involved in that, but the fantastic news is that you are likely to thrive. For starters, your expectations align with the work that accompanies real estate investing. When that happens, you mitigate risk.

Sail Into Your Sunset with a Flush Account

Given the realities of our lives, there is no way around assuming responsibility for our retirement. What I mean by that is that it is in our control how we retire. In some ways, this is a wonderful opportunity for us. We can become true investors. This demands that we have a plan and become deep thinkers versus relying on either Social Security or on others making investment decisions for us. We create our lives, no one else. It is our journey and commitment to it that counts.

So, in order to become true real estate investors and to use SD-IRA accounts well, we must:

- Start with what we have and build on it.
- Buy and hold income-generating real estate assets.
- Create our own lives and wealth in all areas of our lives.
- Learn from successful investors in real estate.
- Commit to growth on all levels.
- Develop patience, persistence and tenacity.
- Mitigate investment risk.
- Use our time wisely.
- Live a life worth living.
- Face our fears.

This book helps you achieve financial success and even financial independence for the time when you retire. Its principles, however, apply to all investments and financial planning, whether for your life or for retirement. You probably already know how important it is to have the financial means to pursue and achieve your dreams and your goals.

This specific subject is about becoming a self-directed IRA real estate investor and driven by gaining clarity. The idea is to propel you to action.

We covered the important basics of real estate and real estate investing and talked about the instrument of self-directed IRAs and how they can help you build wealth. Next, we spoke about getting started with real estate investing in a self-directed diary, how to do the homework on any search investment. How to crunch the numbers, how to view the investments, how to manage them and how to stay on the right side of the law.

Real estate investment strategies inside SD-IRA accounts can work for investors who have little cash or for those who are flush. Among strategies that work for those whose accounts are small count wholesaling or optioning properties, investing in notes or becoming a lender. Start with one investment and build on it. You may discover it works so well that other investments become less important or stay on the sidelines. But everything depends on your goals, your baseline, and various other factors.

As you repeat what works, your account will grow. That's exciting!

While the book covers the bases for SD-IRAs, each real estate niche contains more information and expertise. A detailed overview of what is possible aims to inspire you. Start by opening an SD-IRA account today, then build a real estate portfolio for that account. Gain financial growth and independence over time, often much with a much shorter time horizon than expected.

As mentioned previously, the information you read in this book comes from two decades of working in the real estate trenches and being a real estate investor as well. Throughout that time, I made several mistakes and learned from them. I corrected the course I was on in order to thrive thereafter. But the mistakes I made may well allow you to avoid them.

I would like to leave you with something even more important than those stories: no matter what happens, commit to learning, becoming the best person and the best investor you can be, enjoying the fruits of your efforts, and never giving up. All of us make mistakes, but how we approach and correct those mistakes sets us apart.

Victimhood holds us back. Instead, keep the knowledge that our choices are always ours top of mind. That is true even when delegating decision-making to someone else. All we have is what we bring to the table. And that can thrill us and allow us to become wealthy.

Financial wealth through real estate investing in an SD-IRA is the aim of the foregoing pages. Building an income-producing portfolio allows for cash flow in your golden years. The sooner you start, the better. This applies even if you are in your fifties and have less time to grow your nest egg. Obviously, starting early helps us leap toward our dreams, in this case retiring comfortably and in style, but it is better to start late than never.

Whether you start early or late, one important secret to generating wealth is through putting to use what you already have. That, of course, is the principle of leverage. Always ask yourself what you can leverage and how you can get more leverage. This involves understanding what you already have and thinking about how best to use it. You are creating more out of what you have and adding it to your stash. Use retirement funds you already have, add to yearly contributions to your SD-IRA and put those monies to work through any or all of the real estate investments we discussed.

Lay out your blueprint to grow your capital, sizable sums or not. The best way to do this is with the end in mind. Here, that might mean the rate of return for which you aim. Never allow a fear of numbers and finances to stop you. Instead, learn to love the numbers. Love doing the homework. Love the results. Make your blueprint SMART: Specific, Measurable, Attainable results, Tracked.

Open your SD-IRA. Assemble and engage your team. Familiarize yourself with investment options, then locate investment opportunities. Once you identify the right one for yourself, consistently move forward. Eliminate what does not work. Keep and replicate what works.

The magic of investing in real estate in your SD-IRA might delight you. It is a matter of repeating what works, leaving behind what does not. You read about the reasons for this inside these pages. Use them well. Or hire me for a consultation about your specific situation. Please also review this book online or send your testimonial to me at info@sdirarealestateinvesting.com.

May you thrive and may your investments grow!

ACKNOWLEDGEMENTS

Ω

Any book, including this one, comprises many facets and requires a great team. I am indebted to colleagues, whether real estate professionals, attorneys, or other professionals. Most of all, I am grateful to my clients for teaching me (almost) everything I know.

A heartfelt thank you to my research assistant Sarah Ambrosio and to my wonderful editor Steffanie Moyers!

ABOUT THE AUTHOR

Ω

Gabrielle Dahms is a real estate broker, investor, and writer and presenter. She holds a master's in history and loves to research and write, all stemming from a voracious appetite for learning and making a difference in the world. Her publications include in The Real Estate Investor Manuals series' titles, and hundreds of articles and blog posts about real estate and how to invest in real estate. When away from the keyboard, she enjoys nature and travel. She volunteers for causes such as animal welfare, feeding the needy, and a local urban tree planting program.

Ω

Other Services include:

- **Speaking engagements— webinars, events, conferences.**
- **Real estate consultations.**
- **Deal analysis.**
- **Personalized masterplan creation for real estate investors.**

Please send an email with your inquiry to realestatemanuals@gmail.com.

Briefly state your contact details (name, address, phone number, email), what you need and indicate your budget.

Thank you!

Watch for our upcoming real estate webinars and courses.

Get an announcement when they are ready.

Please sign up for the mailing list here

www.sdirarealestateinvesting.com[1]

The promise:

Occasional announcements only.

---

1. http://www.sdirarealestateinvesting.com

Selected Real Estate Investor Resources

FINRA **https://brokercheck.finra.org/** Check out the party you are dealing with on this site.

www.nasaa.org[1] The North American Securities Administration Association

www.irs.gov[2] Contains Publication 590 and a section about scams and how to avoid them

https://www.finra.org/ Financial Industry Regulatory Authority

www.FBI.gov/scams[3] FBI site. Page on scams

https://www.bbb.org/ [4]Better Business Bureau

https://ritaus.org/ [5]Retirement Industry Association

10Bii Financial Calculator App Available on Google Play

https://www.developgoodhabits.com/financial-calculator-apps/

https://www.proapod.com/calculator/free/o_coc.php

Read more about SD-IRA distribution requirements here:

https://www.congress.gov/bill/116th-congress/house-bill/1994/text

https://www.kiplinger.com/article/retirement/t037-c032-s014-secure-act-basics-what-everyone-should-know.html

https://www.investopedia.com/what-is-secure-act-how-affect-retirement-4692743

https://www.forbes.com/sites/jamiehopkins/2021/04/16/required-minimum-distributions-return-in-2021-prepare-for-new-complexities-and-rules/?sh=25dc807f4ae3

Note investing

https://www.safeguardcapitalpartners.com/faq

www.roof4all.com[6]

---

1.   http://www.nasaa.org

2.   http://www.irs.gov

3.   http://www.fbi.gov/scams

4.   https://www.bbb.org/

5.   https://ritaus.org/

www.constlending.com[7]

Non-recourse loans

The Lending Resources Group http://lendingresourcesgroup.com/

First Western Savings Bank www.myiralender.com

North American Savings Bank (NASB) www.nasb.com

https://www.iraresources.com/self-directed-ira/professionals-network

https://www.theentrustgroup.com/investments/real-estate/strategies/non-recourse-loans

Tax liens

https://ustaxlienassociation.com/ Offers a 7-day video course about tax liens.

https://www.investopedia.com/articles/investing/061313/investing-property-tax-liens.asp

https://www.secretsoftaxlieninvesting.com/state-info Membership site with some free training collateral.

National Association of Counties https://www.naco.org/ Fabulous sites for researching housing, demographics, labor, and much else.

https://www.roofstock.com/ SFH turnkey properties – online platform

https://www.propstream.com/ Real estate information and leads

https://www.dealmachine.com/ Investor & wholesaling app

---

6.   http://www.roof4all.com

7.   http://www.constlending.com

Appendix

Custodian Comparison

Download the comparison for your records at www.sdirarealestateinvesting.com[1]

Due diligence checklist

Download the comparison for your records at www.sdirarealestateinvesting.com[2]

ROI Calculator

Download the comparison for your records at www.sdirarealestateinvesting.com[3]

Commercial Lease Agreement – California

Download the comparison for your records at www.sdirarealestateinvesting.com[4]

---

1.   http://www.sdirarealestateinvesting.com

2.   http://www.sdirarealestateinvesting.com

3.   http://www.sdirarealestateinvesting.com

4.   http://www.sdirarealestateinvesting.com

Index

Bibliography

Adam Bergman, Esq. *The Checkbook IRA - Why You Want It, Why You Need It: A Private Conversation with a Top Retirement Tax Attorney*. CreateSpace Independent Publishing Platform, 2015.

Agent, Twila Slesnick PhD Enrolled, and John C. Suttle Attorney. *IRAs, 401(k)s & Other Retirement Plans: Strategies for Taking Your Money Out*. Fifthteen Ediiton edition. NOLO, 2021.

"Put Your Money Where Your Life Is: How to Invest Locally Using Self-Directed IRAs and Solo 401(k)s (Audible Audio Edition): Michael H. Shuman, Sean Pratt, Berrett-Koehler Publishers: Audible Books & Originals."

Bagli, Charles V. *Other People's Money: Inside the Housing Crisis and the Demise of the Greatest Real Estate Deal Ever M Ade*. Reprint edition. New York: Plume, 2014.

Blacharski, Dan W., and Marie Lujanac. *The Part-Time Real Estate Investor: How to Generate Huge Profits While Keeping Your Day Job*. Atlantic Publishing Company, 2007.

Briggman, Salvador, and Krystine Therriault. *Real Estate Crowdfunding Explained: How to Get in on the Explosive Growth of the Real Estate Crowdfunding Industry*. CreateSpace Independent Publishing Platform, 2016.

Cortese, Amy. *Locavesting: The Revolution in Local Investing and How to Profit From It*. 1st edition. Wiley, 2011.

Dorkin, Joshua, and Brandon Turner. *BiggerPockets Presents: The Ultimate Beginner's Guide to Real Estate Investing*. BiggerPockets Publishing, LLC, 2013.

Eldred, Gary W. *Investing in Real Estate*. 7th edition. Hoboken, New Jersey: Wiley, 2012.

Farmer, E. B. *The Land Flipper: Turning Dirt into Dollars*. CreateSpace Independent Publishing Platform, 2016.

Ferguson, Mark. *Build a Commercial Real Estate Empire: How to Scale to New Heights With the Right Financing, Deals, and Strategies*. Edited by Gregory Helmerick. Independently published, 2020.

———. *Build a Rental Property Empire: The No-Nonsense Book on Finding Deals, Financing the Right Way, and Managing Wisely*. Edited by Lynda Pelissier. CreateSpace Independent Publishing Platform, 2016.

Geltner, David M., Norman G. Miller, Jim Clayton, and Piet Eichholtz. *Commercial Real Estate Analysis and Investments*. 2 edition. Mason, Ohio: ONCOURSE LEARNING, 2006.

Graham, Benjamin, Jason Zweig, and Warren E. Buffett. *The Intelligent Investor Rev Ed.: The Definitive Book on Value Investing*. Revised ed. edition. New York: Harper Business, 2006.

Hennessey, Brian. *The Due Diligence Handbook For Commercial Real Estate: A Proven System To Save Time, Money, Headaches And Create Value When Buying Commercial Real Estate*. Second edition. United States: CreateSpace Independent Publishing Platform, 2015.

Johnson, Ben E. *Money Talks, Bullsh*t Walks: Inside the Contrarian Mind of Billionaire Mogul Sam Zell*. Portfolio, 2009.

Keller, Gary, Dave Jenks, and Jay Papasan. *The Millionaire Real Estate Investor*. 1 edition. New York: McGraw-Hill Education, 2005.

Keller, and Papasan. *The ONE Thing: The Surprisingly Simple Truth About Extraordinary Results*. 1st edition. Austin, Texas: Bard Press, 2013.

Lake, L. J. *Seller Financing: Real Estate Investing for Anyone*. Vassar International Publishing, 2015.

Loftis, Larry. *Profit by Investing in Real Estate Tax Liens: Earn Safe, Secured, and Fixed Returns Every Time*. Second edition. New York: Kaplan Publishing, 2007.

McElroy, Ken. *The ABCs of Real Estate Investing: The Secrets of Finding Hidden Profits Most Investors Miss*. Reprint edition. Minden, NV: RDA Press, LLC, 2012.

Rice, Patrick W. *IRA Wealth: Revolutionary IRA Strategies for Real Estate Investment*. Later Printing edition. Garden City Park, NY: Square One, 2003.

Rosen, Kenneth D. *Investing in Income Properties: The Big Six Formula for Achieving Wealth in Real Estate*. 2 edition. Hoboken: Wiley, 2017.

Sorensen, Mat. *The Self-Directed IRA Handbook, Second Edition: An Authoritative Guide For Self Directed Retirement Plan Investors and Their Advisors*. 2nd edition. SOKOH Publishing, 2018.

Spirer, Gary. *Crowdfunding: The Next Big Thing*. North Charleston: CreateSpace Independent Publishing Platform, 2013.

Sr, Richard Desich. *Self-Directed IRAs: Building Retirement Wealth Through Alternative Investing*. Equity University, 2015.

Stein, Mark, and Terry Lewis. *Seller Financing and Real Estate Notes in the Dodd-Frank Era: By Seller Finance Consultants Inc.* Seller Finance Consultants Inc., 2015.

Turner, Brandon. *The Book on Rental Property Investing: How to Create Wealth and Passive Income Through Intelligent Buy & Hold Real Estate Investing!* 1 edition. Denver: BiggerPockets, 2015.

Zell, Sam. *Am I Being Too Subtle?: Straight Talk From a Business Rebel.* Portfolio, 2017.

Zero Risk Real Estate: Creating Wealth Through Tax Liens and Tax Deeds. 1 edition. Wiley, 2012.

End Notes

[i] https://www.investopedia.com/ask/answers/041015/what-rate-return-should-i-expect-my-401k.asp

Also see https://www.cbpp.org/blog/for-most-americans-retirement-accounts-are-paltry

[ii] Inflation stands at 2.4% on average per year. (source)

[iii] https://www.nolo.com/legal-encyclopedia/are-my-retirement-accounts-protected-from-judgment-creditors-california.html

[iv] Robert Kiyosaki is the author of this term.

[v] https://www.irs.gov/pub/irs-pdf/p590.pdf

[vi] https://smartasset.com/retirement/average-retirement-savings-are-you-normal

[vii] https://www.schwab.com/retirement-planning-tools/retirement-calculator, https://www.investor.gov/financial-tools-calculators/calculators/savings-goal-calculator

[viii] https://www.gobankingrates.com/retirement/planning/jaw-dropping-stats-state-retirement-america/

[ix] https://www.census.gov/

[x] Eldred, Gary, Investing in Real Estate, 7th edition, pg. 338.

[xi] https://www.investor.gov/free-financial-planning-tools

[xii] Per the U.S. Census. https://www.census.gov/

[xiii] https://www.forbes.com/sites/impactpartners/2018/02/09/where-did-all-the-pensions-go/?sh=8c3f2bc3aaba

[xiv] https://www.federalreserve.gov/publications/2019-economic-well-being-of-us-households-in-2018-dealing-with-unexpected-expenses.htm

[xv] https://time.com/nextadvisor/banking/savings/us-saving-rate-soaring/

[xvi] https://www.bloomberg.com/opinion/articles/2021-06-17/america-should-become-a-nation-of-renters

[xvii] https://www.globest.com/2020/11/11/were-on-track-to-be-a-renter-nation-again/

[xviii]   https://www.forbes.com/sites/forbesreal   estatecouncil/2020/04/01/america-a-rentership-nation/[1]

[xix] For more information about tax brackets for 2021, please see this article: https://www.forbes.com/advisor/taxes/taxes-federal-income-tax-bracket/

[xx] https://www.investopedia.com/ask/answers/081915/my-iraroth-ira-fdicinsured.asp

[xxi]   https://www.irs.gov/credits-deductions/individuals/earned-income-tax-credit/earned-income-and-earned-income-tax-credit-eitc-tables#Earned%20Income[2]

[xxii] https://www.investopedia.com/roth-and-traditional-ira-contribution-limits-for-2021-5085118

[xxiii] Go to xxx for more information on owning and operating a business in your self-directed IRA.

[xxiv] Rules can change, so stay abreast of IRS amendments to these accounts.

[xxv] https://www.irs.gov/publications/p590b#en_US_2020_publink1000230936

[xxvi] https://www.irs.gov/publications/p590b#en_US_2020_publink100035552

[xxvii] Custodians can be a bank, a trust company, or another authorized entity.

[xxviii]   https://www.investopedia.com/articles/personal-finance/010616/whats-average-401k-balance-age.asp

[xxix] Note here that the percentage of expenses and the percentage of ownership and profits must be the same.

[xxx] Non-recourse debt means that the loan is secured by its collateral, not by the borrower.

[xxxi] Last I checked Whole Foods had 500+ locations in the U.S. The company's stores are in strategic locations, based on extensive research.

[xxxii] https://www.investopedia.com/terms/t/tenancy_in_common.asp

[xxxiii] Tax liens comprise vast subject matter and differ from state to state in lien states. Investors must educate themselves about terms, rates of return, competition, and processes.

[xxxiv]   https://www.investopedia.com/articles/investing/092815/how-become-accredited-investor.asp

[xxxv] https://www.irs.gov/pub/irs-tege/eotopicn86.pdf

---

1. https://www.forbes.com/sites/forbesrealestatecouncil/2020/04/01/america-a-rentership-nation/

2.   https://www.irs.gov/credits-deductions/individuals/earned-income-tax-credit/earned-income-and-earned-income-tax-credit-eitc-tables#Earned_0bcef9c45bd8a48eda1b26eb0c61c869_20Income

[xxxvi] https://www.nolo.com/legal-encyclopedia/state-state-seller-disclosure-requirements

[xxxvii] A scheme in which investors get paid with funds from new investors coming in but in which the money is not invested and instead used to pay the fraudster and prior investors. Promises of high returns and low or no risk are signature imprints. Ponzi schemes eventually collapse but the money is gone at that point.

[xxxviii] Registered investments provide information about investment management,

[xxxix] https://www.sec.gov/tcr

Did you love *Investing in Real Estate in Your Self-Directed IRA*? Then you should read *The Art and Science of Real Estate Negotiation*[3] by Gabrielle Dahms!

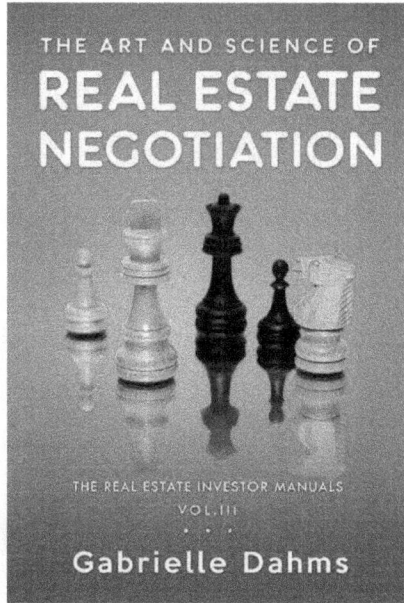

The Sky's the Limit!

The Art and Science of Real Estate Negotiation addresses a practice that is indispensable to real estate success: negotiation. Negotiation principles and fundamentals affect real estate buyers, sellers, and investors in getting results. This may include buying or selling a home or investing in much larger real estate deals.

Read this book and be(come) a powerful real estate investor who nets **results and dollars.** You well may also find that what you read improves your everyday communications outside of real estate.

The Art and Science of Real Estate Negotiation is the third volume in **The Real Estate Investor Manuals.**

3. https://books2read.com/u/mBo2DR

4. https://books2read.com/u/mBo2DR

It draws upon the author's knowledge base and her 20-year experience as a real estate professional and a real estate investor.

So why not hone your skills with knowledge and experience captured in this book written by an industry veteran?

Topics include:

Real estate-specific negotiating.Negotiation principles.The real estate negotiation process.How to establish rapport.Discerning the other party's motivation.Solve problems. Get results.Negotiation strategies and tactics.Avoiding negotiation traps and pitfalls.And much, much more...

Whether you want to be a better negotiator, close more real estate deals, or increase your bottom line, this book is for you!

Read it now!

Read more at https://www.BooksmartPress.com.

Also by Gabrielle Dahms

The Real Estate Investor Manuals
How Trends Make You A Smarter Investor
Finding Profitable Deals
The Art and Science of Real Estate Negotiation
Investing in Real Estate in Your Self-Directed IRA

Watch for more at https://www.BooksmartPress.com.

www.ingramcontent.com/pod-product-compliance
Lightning Source LLC
Chambersburg PA
CBHW022102210326
41518CB00039B/377